Jesus for Life

Jesus for Life

Spiritual Readings in John's Gospel

Richard S. Briggs

CASCADE *Books* • Eugene, Oregon

JESUS FOR LIFE
Spiritual Readings in John's Gospel

Copyright © 2019 Richard S. Briggs. All rights reserved. Except for brief quotations in critical publications or reviews, no part of this book may be reproduced in any manner without prior written permission from the publisher. Write: Permissions, Wipf and Stock Publishers, 199 W. 8th Ave., Suite 3, Eugene, OR 97401.

Cascade Books
An Imprint of Wipf and Stock Publishers
199 W. 8th Ave., Suite 3
Eugene, OR 97401

www.wipfandstock.com

PAPERBACK ISBN: 978-1-5326-6724-4
HARDCOVER ISBN: 978-1-5326-6725-1
EBOOK ISBN: 978-1-5326-6726-8

Cataloguing-in-Publication data:

Names: Briggs, Richard S., author.

Title: Jesus for life : spiritual readings in John's Gospel / by Richard S. Briggs.

Description: Eugene, OR: Cascade Books, 2019

Identifiers: ISBN 978-1-5326-6724-4 (paperback) | ISBN 978-1-5326-6725-1 (hardcover) | ISBN 978-1-5326-6726-8 (ebook)

Subjects: LCSH: Bible. John—Commentaries.

Classification: LCC BS2615.3 B78 2019 (print) | LCC BS2615.3 (ebook)

Scripture quotations are from New Revised Standard Version Bible, copyright © 1989 National Council of the Churches of Christ in the United States of America. Used by permission. All rights reserved worldwide.

Manufactured in the U.S.A.   07/12/19

To Alan

A man committed to grace and truth

Contents

Acknowledgments | ix

Introduction—Reading for Life | 1
A Prayer For Our Reading of John's Gospel | 8

1. Finding Our Identity in the Beginning—John 1 | 9
2. Behold, the Lamb of God—John 1 | 16
3. Mary Takes Her Son to a Wedding... —John 2 | 25
4. True Love, or "What John 3:16 Really Means" —John 3 | 33
5. Encounter at the Well—John 4 | 45
6. Walking on the Water of the New Creation—John 6 | 51
7. Not Dead Yet—John 11 | 57
8. Jesus Gives Himself Away—John 13 | 65
9. Learning from Philip How Not to Understand —John 14 | 73
10. Beyond the Dying of the Light: Resurrection —John 20 | 81

Concluding Reflection—An Essay on Spiritual Reading and John | 91

Closing Credits—In Others' Words | 104

Acknowledgments

I AM GRATEFUL TO attentive gatherings and congregations who have listened to various versions of some of the chapters included here, in particular to the good people of St. Mary's Sherburn, St. Cuthbert's Shadforth, and St. Giles, Gilesgate, in England's glorious North East, where I was privileged to be serving as a curate during the writing of this book. I shall be delighted if the results help to nourish and sustain them in enjoying the word of life. Other original settings have included gatherings of the faithful in Cranmer Hall, Durham, and in King's Church, Durham.

I am in particular grateful to Aian and Kia Macpherson for an invitation a few years ago to speak at their son Nathanael's baptism, and for choosing John 1 for their text, which started me thinking about trying to read John for a word of life. Aian has also given generous, detailed, and thoughtful feedback on the whole book, as have both Andy Byers and Melody Briggs (the latter of whom greatly enjoyed the chance to scribble question marks and exclamation marks over her husband's manuscript). I am indebted to all three of them for helping me to avoid various unhelpful ways of putting things, and apologize for not following even more

ACKNOWLEDGMENTS

of their advice. Other gracious readers helping me to see how these readings looked from other perspectives included Matt and Katie Lawrence, Walter Moberly, Jenn Riddlestone, and on the concluding reflection in particular, Mike Higton. I thank them all, while happily acknowledging that none of them are responsible for any errors or wayward opinions that follow. Finally, I am grateful to Philip Plyming for initially prompting me to write this book, and to Chris Spinks for giving it a home within the wonderfully encouraging world of Cascade Books.

It is my pleasure to dedicate these reflections to my long-time colleague, friend, and lately my training incumbent too: Alan Bartlett. Alan has facilitated my own work in God's church through his patient and loving ministry in Gilesgate, Sherburn, and Shadforth, as well as more widely around Durham. I hope that this book bears some of the hallmarks of his own wisdom and insight.

Richard Briggs
St Mary's Church, Sherburn
Festival of the Birth of Mary, 2018

Introduction

Reading for Life

THERE ARE MANY WAYS to read the Bible. Not all of them are helpful.

Of course, how you should read the Bible depends on why you want to read the Bible. Perhaps your interest is in ancient history, or great literature, or the source of theological doctrines. All of those are fair interests. Perhaps your interest is in proving that you are right, or discovering never-before-seen confirmation of the latest theories about human follies and flourishing. These are less likely to be constructive interests for Bible reading, but what with it being the social media age and the opportunity to pursue self-expression being mysteriously turned into an untamed virtue, you will be able to go a long way with those interests too—though this is probably not the book for you. (Or, on second thought, maybe it is exactly the book you should read.)

What if you want to read the Bible to hear a word of life? What if your wager is that there is a God; and not just that there is a God, but there is a God who has revealed something important—indeed, has disclosed something fundamental about God's identity—in Jesus? Furthermore, what if this God has brought it about that we have before us some written Gospel records that lead us, truthfully and life-givingly, to that self-revealing?

If that is you, then whether or not you are right (I would say you are), that certainly sets up an interesting way to read the Bible: reading it for the word of life, known most fully in Jesus Christ, but reflected and refracted through the written word of Holy Scripture. In turn, this word of life is further spread abroad throughout the land (indeed the world) by way of countless preached sermons in gatherings of the faithful, week by week. To see things this way is to set oneself up to read the word of God. What a privilege. What a responsibility. And what an invitation: to come and read.

The world is not short of people taking up the invitation. At the same time, one has to say, a lot of such reading is not always well focused on locking in to that word of life. It gets a little lost among the details, or the moral exhortation, or the hundred-and-one other worthwhile things that crowd in on human reading. In the twenty-first century, to borrow Alan Jacobs's wonderful characterization, we are in pursuit of the pleasures of reading in the age of distraction.

Christian reading of Scripture is not immune to this distraction, nor to multiple ways of missing the word of life, even in the most well-intentioned readings (or sermons). There is a time and a place for theoretical books discussing the vexed question of how to read the Bible "properly," or "well," or "in context," and so on. Such books will often say that they are about "hermeneutics"—the science or art of handling the interpretation of the (biblical) text. I have myself written one or two books like that. But here I want simply to head out into the biblical text and read it, in pursuit of life.

INTRODUCTION

I think it might be useful to call this approach "spiritual reading." Spiritual reading is—or can be—enabled by the Spirit, in search of the Spirit's illumination, and above all, out of all the many, many good lines of enquiry that one can pursue with the biblical text, it seeks a word of life. It is not necessarily a word of moral teaching, or exhortation, or energetic encouragement, or enthusiasm, or vaguely related spiritual aspiration, though perhaps all those things will creep in as we read. I have certainly heard Bible readers reporting enthusiastic and spiritually aspirational things after reading the Bible, where I have wondered whether those things had much to do with the Bible passage they had been reading. This is not the worst problem in the world, so a certain sense of perspective is appropriate before criticizing it too much. After all—and as a common example—being nice to people is better than a lot of the alternatives, and if you think the Bible passage you are reading is encouraging you to be nice, then that is unlikely to be a disaster. But on the other hand, it may well make it harder to see just how the passage in question offers a Christ-shaped word of life, which would undoubtedly offer much more in the way of blessing, hope, and—in the end—truth.

I could go on at length (at great length) about other reflections on what counts as reading for life, and what spiritual reading really is or is not. But instead, the best path here is to engage in it, and to learn by doing.

Reading John

To carry out these exercises in spiritual reading, we need some Bible texts. In this book, they all come from the

Gospel of John. Occasionally, it is illuminating to read one Bible passage alongside another one to see how they shed light on each other. In particular, Gospel passages often presume that their readers know something of the Old Testament. Sometimes, I suggest and explore an Old Testament passage to read alongside the reading from John. But John is basically the focus.

Perhaps I should confess that, although I love the Gospel of John, it has not generally been my favorite book of the Bible, and is certainly not the book I find easiest to read. I tend to find reading Luke, or some of the great stories of the Old Testament, a bit more straightforward, at least on a first read through. But in various contexts over the years, I have been required to engage with John, and this has had an interesting effect. I have had to work hard, and dig deep, to get anywhere at all. Arguably, as a result, I have been forced to read with more disciplined focus on the possibilities of finding a word of life in these texts. I certainly think I have found life. Readers will perhaps want to reflect on how far this life is Christ-shaped and faithful to the God of Holy Scripture.

This is not a commentary on John, nor is it a comprehensive study of John. Most obviously, I read only a few passages. The selection of a passage does not mean it is more important than another passage that is omitted. I wanted this to be a short book—an invitation to read spiritually, rather than a full apprenticeship. There is always more: further passages, and also further reflections on the passages that are included. I hope that readers who are helped will themselves go on and read further.

In the spirit of reading first and theorizing later, I am not going to spend any time here in the introduction

INTRODUCTION

giving background information on John and his Gospel. There are various benefits to this strategy, not least because, in my judgment, we actually know rather little about the background of John and his Gospel. I have read quite a few theories about such background issues, and it seems very likely that at least one of them is true. If we knew which one it was, I would tell you.

More broadly, though, there is a strange idea at work when we think that background information is a necessary preparation for reading a good book. Now, it might be, on occasion. It depends on the book. With the Gospel of John, I am tempted to think that the only really important pieces of background information you need are that it is one of the four Gospels that made it into the Christian Bible; that it is quite unlike the other three; and that the word "gospel" means "good news," so that the Gospel of John is, as it were, the good news according to John. In particular, it is good news about Jesus Christ. Armed with this short introduction, I think you are ready to jump in and read John and see what happens.

Readers who would like more—more theory, more background, and more chances to enjoy other kinds of reading that are not particularly attempting to be spiritual readings—are invited to take up the essay at the end of the book, which points to various ways of thinking about all these other issues. As for me, admitting that I am a reader who spends a great deal of time exploring just that kind of further reading, the more difficult challenge for myself is the attempt to read the biblical text in a disciplined way that tries to stay attuned to the word of life, or to spiritual reading. In short: there is no better way to pursue the practice of spiritual reading than to engage in it.

One thing this does mean, as we proceed, is that you will get much more out of this book if you always read the Bible passages listed first before going on to read the reflections in this book. So turn with me to John chapter 1, and let us begin.

A Prayer For Our Reading of John's Gospel

Lord God

we thank you for the strange but wonderful gift of Holy Scripture.

Give us open eyes and open ears

open hearts and open minds

to be summoned and shaped by your word of life,

that it might take root in us

and bear fruit in our lives.

Amen.

CHAPTER 1

Finding our Identity in the Beginning—John 1

Read John 1:1–18, 43–51

JOHN'S GOSPEL DOES NOT begin with a funny story. Did you notice that?

What was John thinking? Isn't everyone supposed to begin with a funny story? Sometimes it is the only part of a sermon worth hearing. I can still recall one occasion when I was an undergraduate, about 180 years ago, when the visiting preacher opened up with an epic and complicated joke about a man in a fridge. I can still tell that joke. I can also remember that after about ten minutes, which is a long time in a public space, he delivered the punchline, let the laughter die down, and then said "Well that has nothing to do with the rest of my sermon." I cannot remember a word, not one word, of what he then went on to say.

But John's Gospel does not begin with a funny story.

Do you think he tried out a few possibilities?

> So I was at this wedding, and we had run out of wine, and you would not believe what happened next . . .

or

> It was a dark and stormy night. And the captain said to the first mate, "There's a man out there walking on the water!" And do you know what, there was!

Or is this a deliberate choice? Does John have very good reasons why he does not want to begin his Gospel with a long anecdote about a man in a fridge, and not just because he does not want that to be the only bit people remember eight or 180 or 1800 years later? "John's Gospel, that's the one with the story about the fridge isn't it?" (I would just like to make clear at this point, for the benefit of those who have never read it, that there is in fact no mention of a fridge in John's Gospel, nor indeed the whole Bible. I hope that is not news to anyone.)

But John's Gospel takes no time in building up to its big point. John does not warm you up gently. He does not even give us a handle on who is telling us what is going on, or when they wrote it, or in fact any kind of context at all, because no context can be big enough for the claim that John wants to begin with: "In the beginning was the Word."

That's it. His Gospel comes straight in with a massive and extraordinary claim about how, or when, or perhaps in whom, everything began. "In the beginning was the Word." Which Word is he talking about? He goes on: "and the Word was with God, and the Word was God." We have just reached the end of the first sentence, and John has made a claim as big as the whole history of the universe: the Word was God. Now it *will* take him a few more sentences to get to the point where he says "the Word became flesh and lived among us," or as one wonderful translation puts it: "the Word became flesh and blood, and moved into the neighborhood" (v. 14, MSG). By this time, barely a few sentences into his Gospel, we now have the claim that everything started with, starts with, and depends on Jesus.

I do not think this is really a claim about the history of how the world began. I suspect John knew that he did not know much about that. Rather, it is a claim about how we should understand everything, and John means *everything*: Jesus is like a light that shines in the darkness, and allows us to see everything in a new way. For everyone coming into the world, Jesus—we read in verse 9—is the true light. He always has been, because he was there in the beginning.

Now John knew, I am sure, that this was not obvious. It still is not obvious. Who looks around the world we live in and says, "Ah yes, of course, clearly Jesus was God in the beginning, and enlightens us all, hearts and minds, and overcomes the darkness"? So perhaps John pondered how to put this point, how to break it gently to his readers that, if you want to understand what is going on in life, in our world, then you need to think about the fact that Jesus is like a light that allows us to see the world that we live in differently. Maybe John tried to say, in an earlier draft, "You all know what a light is like, right? How when you flick the switch it transforms the room you are in and helps you see what you could not see before? Well, Jesus is a bit like that." Except, of course, that they did not have light switches then, so maybe he was a bit puzzled about how to explain how this light came into the world. Maybe he thought he could tell the whole baby-in-the-manger-in-the-stable story, but Matthew and Luke had already published their versions, and he was inclined to think that he could not top that, and anyway the baby Jesus was not really the point, because the point, really, was as big as the whole history of the world, and affected everything, and was so wonderful that you could not contain it in a story about Mary and Joseph, or John the Baptist (though, come to think of it, that bit might still be useful, and maybe he could still work it in). You really needed a perspective as big as *everything* to get the sense of what Jesus means, and then: "Aha!" John gets it. "This is the way to begin: *In the beginning* was the Word."

Later on he decides to go back and edit in the additional information that the Word was Jesus (basically).

No, John's Gospel does not begin with a funny story, because there is nowhere to start the story other than with God. With Christ. In the beginning.

Is John saying that if you start there, then you might begin to make sense of everything else? There might be light enough to understand the life that you live, and the world that you live it in. On the other hand, if you do not start there, you will never be able to reach the point where you sit back in your rocking chair and reflect: "You know, I think I have finally worked out how to fit Jesus into my picture of how it all works." Because, John seems to say, it is not possible to fit Jesus into your picture. You cannot build up to making sense of him. You cannot work yourself up to being good enough to meet God on equal terms, and say, "I think we can do a deal here: I will let you run Sundays and summer camp, while I look after Saturdays and take care of the finances." No, you start with Jesus and fit everything else in around him. (This turns out to involve a lot of fine wine and fish suppers, among other things, so it is not perhaps as gloomy as it might sound at first; but that would be another story.)

For all these reasons, John does not start with a funny story, but with Christ: Christ over all, before all, in all, shining like a light in the darkness; indeed, *the* light in the darkness, without whom we will not really see what is going on. Is it possible to have a more basic point about beginnings than this? Well, perhaps there was that attempt long ago to make another really basic point about beginnings: "In the beginning, when God created the heavens and the earth," back in Genesis 1:1, the very start of the whole Bible. Of course, John is echoing that verse and saying that, after all, it turns out to be about Christ too. I think John would say that, in the light of Christ, we are now in a position to go back and reread Genesis, and really understand that properly too.

Think now about our own lives and our own beginnings. The idea of saying that we have to begin with Christ and fit the rest of life around him is basically what is going on when we decide to let God mark the beginning of our lives in Christian baptism. For some, this is a conscious decision later in life to "begin again." For others, it takes place in a context of a Christian family, wanting to mark a new life for Christ. In such cases, parents do not say, "Why not get someone in to tell a few funny stories. We will all drink a toast, see what happens as our little girl (or boy) grows up, and if they decide that they have made enough sense of things one day to want to follow Jesus, then they could decide to get baptized, and we could always have another get-together then." Rather, it is precisely because they care about their daughter's (or son's) life and how they will live it and make sense of it, that they want it to begin with Jesus.

Marking a baby's new life in baptism is a profound statement of theological confidence in the God who seriously proposes that there is no other beginning than in Christ. In my own tradition, parents, godparents, indeed any who celebrate on such an occasion, are invited to say, in response to some questions about God the Father, God the Son, and God the Holy Spirit, that they "believe and trust in him." There are comparable questions and affirmations in most Christian traditions, in fact. Several times, one may hear these words repeated: "We believe and trust in him." It is not that we understand him and have got everything worked out, but simply that we believe and trust in him. The baby in question does not understand what is going on. They do not have it all worked out, and of course neither do the parents. Nor do any of us. But what we can say, and what we are invited to say, is "We believe and trust in him." In starting there, there is some hope that the rest of life might make a little more sense in the light that God provides.

What does that look like? In practice, what does it mean to start with Jesus and then learn how to see life with God more clearly? Surely it is no coincidence that, in these opening sections of John's Gospel, John moves on quite quickly to give some examples of people who "start with Jesus" and then move on towards insight and understanding. Thus it is not long in this opening chapter of John's Gospel before we encounter various people who sign up to follow Jesus: in particular, Philip and Nathanael, in verses 43–51. Note that they too do not really know where they are going or what their life is going to look like. Nathanael does not understand who Jesus is, but Jesus knows who Nathanael is, and blesses him in a range of ways that will one day make a lot more sense to him. Nathanael's first meeting with Jesus here, we might say, is a model for all of us who follow along, as we come to meet Jesus too.

We sometimes say that we are invited to live Jesus-shaped lives. But perhaps we should also say that we are invited to live Nathanael-shaped lives. Because we too hope that we will set out on lives in which things will begin to make a lot more sense to us, and that like Nathanael we might come to be people "in whom there is no deceit" (v. 47). But most of all, we are invited to live Nathanael-shaped lives in the sense that we are invited to find our identity, in Christ, in the beginning. That is basically what the language of "baptismal identity" means, and it applies to any Christian life, whether marked at the beginning by starting with baptism, or marked in the sense of a new start—later on—in baptism for those whose earthly days do not begin here. In the joy of new beginning, it can be possible to get carried away with unrealistic hopes that all will now be well. But there is a startling mix of realism and genuine hopefulness in the way Christians are invited to live out life's highs and lows. We *will* face trouble in this life, as John's Gospel goes on to say later (16:33). But take heart, because we are baptized into Christ, and Christ has overcome the darkness.

CHAPTER 2

Behold, the Lamb of God—John 1

Read John 1:29–42 (and Isaiah 49:1–7)

THIS SECTION OF JOHN 1, and the accompanying passage of Isaiah, are often read during the season of Epiphany. Epiphany means "seeing," "beholding," or as I like to think of it, "getting the point." Epiphany season, following Christmas season, is about Jesus being made clear to us. There in verse 29 is John the Baptist, saying "Here is the Lamb of God." But "here is" is not simply a marker of location, or meeting. It is the good old-fashioned exclamation "Behold!" This word "behold" functioned like saying "will you look at that!" and was designed to make sure you did not miss what was being described. "Behold the Lamb of God . . . who takes away the sin of the world."

The next thing John the Baptist says, "This is he of whom I said" (v. 30), is a bit obscure, since it seems to refer to Jesus' baptism, and rather oddly John does not tell us about Jesus' baptism. Perhaps he is assuming that we have read the other Gospels first? In those Gospels (Matt 3:13–17; Mark 1:9–11; Luke 3:21–22), Jesus is baptized by John in the river Jordan, and the Holy Spirit descends on Jesus in the form of a dove. Here in John, we simply read John

BEHOLD, THE LAMB OF GOD—JOHN 1

saying that he was told to look out for the one on whom the Spirit descended. (I think this must mean that God told him this, though admittedly it is not entirely clear.) Then John saw the dove, and so he realized *that Jesus was the Son of God*. If there is any value in using "epiphany" language, then this is surely one of the things we should be "seeing," that is made clear to us each Epiphany: Jesus is the Son of God. Furthermore, he is sent by the Father and—according to this passage—baptized by the Holy Spirit. That is the whole Trinity right here in this one passage. So all we need to do now is explain the Holy Trinity and we are sorted? On second thoughts, let us try a different route.

Consider instead the Old Testament, and in particular the great prophet Isaiah. There is so much going on in Isaiah, even just in Isaiah 49, that there is no way to do more than pick out one or two key issues that will help us read John. (Keep an eye out, as we go through this book, for how often a good grasp of the Old Testament can be helpful for reading the Gospels). Isaiah 49 begins with a bit of poetic setting-up for a couple of verses, calling everyone to order—though admittedly "everyone" appears to be the whole surrounding world—and then describing the speaker, whose specific identity is left a bit vague. Then in verse 3 we come to a startling but wonderful claim: "He said to me 'You are my servant, Israel, in whom I will be glorified.'" What does it mean for God to say that Israel is his servant? For how long has this been true? According to the references to "the womb" in verses 1 and 5, and the mention of "before I was born" in verse 1, Israel has always been God's servant, since "before they were born," as it were. If this sounds a bit confusing, it might help to think of the king or the prophet speaking on behalf of Israel at this point.

Now the key thing about this Isaiah passage is the next bit, beginning with "It is too light a thing" (verse 6). Here God tells Israel what they were originally going to do, and what he now wants them to do instead, or as well. What is it? In the never-bettered words of this ancient prophet Isaiah, the calling for God's people is to be "a light to the nations," across the whole earth.

Consider what is being claimed here: the story of the history of the whole world according to Isaiah. In the beginning, God created Israel. It did take a few chapters of Genesis to get this project underway, but it is well and truly on track by about a quarter of the way through Genesis. What Isaiah wants us to grasp is what he sees as the most basic thing about God's relationship with Israel: God loves them. God did not choose them because they had it all sorted out, any more than each of us as individuals has it all sorted out, as we saw in the previous chapter. Neither did God choose them because they were particularly hard-working compared to other nations, or the most impressive leaders, or the best choral tradition, even though they did have one: singing the Psalms in their worship. Very simply, God chose them because he loved them, and he loved them because—well, he just loved them.

The second most important thing about God's love for Israel is that God wanted it to spill over into a love for everyone else. (Christian readers sometimes give the impression that this was the most important thing, but that is a regrettable way of understanding the value or significance of a love that overflows its initial focus, as if the initial focus—Israel in this case—was not equally important.) This second point is exactly what Isaiah is saying here. On the one hand, God's servant has their hands full raising up the tribes of Jacob and restoring the survivors of Israel. A little historical context here: Isaiah is probably saying this during the exile, when Israel has been scattered among the nations. We are talking about the sixth century BCE. Things are not going well, as the Babylonians are in charge; hence this call to raise up and restore God's people. But then, on the other hand, at just the moment when you could be forgiven for thinking that Israel had enough to worry about, God adds this: "I will give you as a light to the nations, that my salvation may reach to the ends of the earth" (49:6).

This is the job of God's servant. To fast forward a bit, Isaiah will go on to say that his servant will suffer for this calling, which is why we call Isaiah's description of this, in Isaiah 53, the "suffering servant," and in that passage of Scripture, let us note, Isaiah writes about the suffering servant who was "like a lamb that is led to the slaughter." In due course, he says that his Spirit will be poured out on his servant, whose job it will be to bring good news to the oppressed (this is now Isaiah 61). You may recall that Jesus reads that bit of Isaiah when he is speaking in the synagogue, and he applies it to himself (Luke 4:16–21). So it turns out that all these ways that Isaiah is describing the calling of God's servant—to restore Israel and to be a light to the nations—apply to Jesus. Then furthermore, just in case you were sitting comfortably, it turns out that it now applies to us. The job description is the same—restore God's people, be a light to the nations—and it applies down through the ages to Israel in and around the sixth century BCE, to the suffering servant, to Jesus, and to us, by which I

19

mean the church. Readers today might helpfully think of this as one way of understanding why the church is here: to be a light to the nations. Conveniently, God sometimes intervenes by delivering the nations right to one's own door. Easy as it can be to despair of the nature and scale of immigration and emigration across our troubled world today, it does give pause for thought about the job-description of being "a light to the nations." For most people in the West today, it has become possible to do part of the work of being a light to the nations while still staying at home, since people of many nations often live in any one town or city. More generally, wherever we are, and whatever we are doing in our lives for God, we are part of God's calling that goes back to Jesus, back to Isaiah, back all the way to Genesis.

Now we are ready to come back to John the Baptist, with his cry: "Behold the lamb of God who takes away the sin of the world" (John 1:29). At least in part this is a reference to that passage in Isaiah 53 that we mentioned: the lamb sent to the slaughter who was the suffering servant, for the sake of the whole world. In other words, John agrees with Isaiah, and says, "Look! (Behold!) This is happening right in front of your eyes, in Jesus." (He wants them to *see* this, which we recall was the point of our "Epiphany" language.)

But what does it mean that Jesus takes away the sin of the world? Sin can be understood in many ways: the good things we have not done and the bad things we have done. It is imagined variously in the Bible as like a burden that we carry, or like a debt that we owe. It is a kind of failure. It is the presence of evil in our world. It can be pride; or selfishness; or greed; and it does not have to be massive examples of any of those things for it to be sin. It is everywhere. It is like dust in your house, or weeds in your garden. It is as dependable as death and taxes, and about as uplifting as well.

In response to this, what John the Baptist is saying, what John's Gospel is saying, and what the Christian Church has always been saying is simply this: Jesus takes it away. He does not just provide a temporary fix, or a quick clean; but he takes the world apart and puts it back together again whole. Or to use the Bible's language: He enters into the heart of the old creation, and turns it into the new creation. He takes the very air that we breathe, and he fills it with the Holy Spirit. If we pay particular attention to our passage from John 1, we might well note the interesting feature that the Spirit remains on Jesus, and Jesus baptizes with the Holy Spirit, which I take to mean that he generously and graciously fills us with the Holy Spirit he has himself received.

Behold the lamb of God, who takes away the sin of the world. Problem solved.

Now all of this is true, but obviously it has proved to be a bit more complicated to work it out over the centuries between then and now.

It turns out that there continues to be sin in the world, and so not everything is perfect from day 1 when we live the Christian life. However, the important point is a simple point: we are not the ones who can take away sin. We are not the ones who can fix the world we live in. Surely we are surrounded by plenty of evidence that that is true: we only have to watch the news and/or follow politics in our twenty-first-century world. If we are waiting until we are good enough for God, we will be waiting a long time. But we are not, because it is Jesus, and not us, who takes our burdens, pays our debts, and makes all things new. Being a Christian is not about doing enough good things to make ourselves right with God, and that is good news, because we never finally do enough good things. Being a Christian is about recognizing that Jesus makes us right with God. That is why John cries, "Behold! The lamb of God."

You might want to ponder how we are supposed to say "thank you" for that. Everything we do for God is a response to the fact that Jesus has taken away sin. We celebrate this, for example, every time we take communion. To borrow some of the language of the standard communion prayers that churches pray, we do not take bread and wine to try and make ourselves right with God, but in thankfulness that Jesus has made us right with God, by taking away our sin. We are invited to respond with praise and worship, and to share in Christ's meal—a meal that is known in many churches as the "eucharistic" meal, since the word "eucharist" means "thanksgiving" (as used by Jesus himself in Luke 22:19, when he gives thanks for the bread at the last supper).

I have one other reflection to offer, and it goes back to the one time I cheated in school. Now I should say that I did many things wrong in school, including being mean to people, and forgetting things I should have done, so without difficulty I could end up confessing a long list of my sins in this context. On the whole, cheating would not be on that list, except once, in swimming classes (which I hated). For everyone else, this was a highpoint of the week: a bus ride to the leisure center, away from the terrors of mathematics and English and science, and a chance to have fun in the water for an hour. But I could not swim, and I hated trying to learn. So each week my heart would sink as we entered the bus and were driven to the pool, and for some reason they always seemed to be playing the Bee Gees singing "How deep is your love?" over the speaker during the journey, which simply caused my mind to drift towards wondering how deep was the pool. Whenever I hear this song, even today, I start to dread my swimming lesson.

In any case, the school wanted everyone to pass their swimming confidence certificate. This was not an overly taxing level to reach, and basically required the young swimmer to be able to get in the water (I could do that), and swim five meters to the side of the pool. I could not do that. My solution, as we moved towards the week where I was the only one left who had not obtained their confidence certificate, was to shuffle as near as I could to the side, and then rely on the fact that I am very tall, and half jump and half fall towards the side of the pool. A particularly inattentive instructor saw me do this and said "That will do," and there I was with my swimming confidence certificate. But the one thing I never had in swimming was confidence, at least until years later, when I finally cracked it.

What I never did was jump in the deep end. Instead I grew up with an unhealthy fear of everything that could go wrong. I realized this when our daughter was four years old, and we enrolled her in a summer swimming course. On day one, as I sat worried by the side of the pool, they threw her in the water, and down she went, and then immediately up she came, giggling, and splashing and clearly already loving it. She has been a confident swimmer ever since.

Why do I tell this story, apart from to confess my sin, with confession being good for the soul? I sometimes think that we approach the Christian life too much like I approached swimming, thinking that if we just get a little bit

23

wet, we could shuffle along, lunge for the side of the pool, and get away with looking like we are doing it, but not really doing it. But actually we need to approach it the way my daughter learned swimming: jump in fully and trust that God/the water will lift you up. If Christianity does not make much sense to us, is it because we have tried to turn it into a spare-time hobby of being religious, doing just enough good to keep God happy? Except that never works. Is that why—when Israel was worrying about the exile and had enough problems of its own—God chose exactly that moment to tell them he had an even bigger job for them, to be a light to the nations?

Lord, we cannot cope! How are we going to manage that? At which point God says, "At last—now we are getting somewhere." Because it was never we ourselves who were going to make it work. Behold the Lamb of God. Jesus takes away the sin of the world. Let us jump in.

CHAPTER 3

Mary Takes Her Son to a Wedding... —John 2

Read John 2:1–12

WHERE IS JESUS LEADING us, and what is Jesus doing? Often we do not know.

How can this be? For many of us, we have known him for a long time, and yet sometimes all we seem able to do in our lives as God's people is to say, "Lord, we are in trouble, we need help, we are out of ideas." That is more or less where Mary finds herself early on in John chapter 2: "Jesus, we are in trouble. They need help, for they are out of wine."

At such times, when the future is unclear, as it so often is, we need the courage to go forward in faith. We also need to hear Mary's words from this story, as she says to some worried servants: "Do whatever he tells you." They do so, and extraordinary things happen. The best, it turns out, is yet to come. Like all stories in John's Gospel, the question arises: is this a story about all of us today, as much as it is about a wedding that Jesus once attended in Cana of Galilee? Let us hear the story carefully, then, before reflecting on how it might speak to us.

Once upon a time, there was a wedding, and Jesus and his mother attended. One of my great privileges in Christian ministry is to officiate wedding services. When I do so, there is a line that typically occurs early on in the service, as part of the explanation of why we are gathered together in a Christian church to celebrate two people joining their lives together. You may recall hearing it if you have attended such wedding services: "Our Lord Jesus Christ was himself a guest at a wedding in Cana of Galilee." The point is simple: Jesus is involved in people's daily lives, attending and taking part in their celebrations. He was invited, and he went along.

Then the wine ran out. At this point, Mary turns to Jesus and says, "They have no wine." Now I can imagine that a mother attending a wedding with her young adult son might be slightly nervous about asking him to get involved. Those of you who have ever had the experience of being accompanied by a teenage son as you went to a wedding may well reflect ruefully on the emotional stress of leaning across the table and saying, "I think they've run out of people to help, would you mind just lending a hand with the washing up?" Is it possible to imagine the son being slightly grumpy in reply?

Oddly enough, that is more or less what seems to happen here. Jesus says, a bit bluntly, "Woman, what concern is that to you and to me?" Translations have always struggled to capture this odd reply in straightforward English. Let me paraphrase it: "Mo-o-om; you're so embarrassing, it's nothing to do with us."

But Mary is persistent. Of course, it is hard to imagine what it must have been like to have a son who sometimes seemed to be shaping up for a public ministry unlike any other; a son who had been such a remarkable, even miraculous, gift in the first place; a son whom she could not easily understand. Indeed, we read of occasions in the Gospels where she is left feeling (and being treated) just like an outsider. But here she seems to hold her nerve, believing that, despite his slightly grumpy-sounding reply, on this occasion her son is going to sort out the problem. So she says, to the people serving at the wedding, "Do whatever he tells you."

Taking stock at this point in the story, note that she has—and we have—no idea what he will tell them. It is unclear how Jesus can or will help, and it is a bit odd to imagine that the forthcoming savior of the world is being pressed into action over a shortage of wine at a wedding. Even allowing for the fact that weddings were lengthy and socially important occasions, and that the absence of wine might spell social embarrassment if not disaster for the hosting family, is this really the arena of Jesus' ministry, to supply drinks? But that is what Jesus does.

Jesus indicates six (very) large stone jars holding water for purification rituals, and tells them to fill the jars with water and then to draw some out to taste it. Honestly, like with most miraculous events in the Gospels, we do not actually get to find out exactly what happened and how. The interest never seems to be in dwelling on the details of what Jesus has done. The interest is in recognizing that he has done it. The water has become wine, and not just any wine, but the best wine. A huge, overflowing amount of it. And they all drank happily ever after.

The servants in the story follow Mary's advice, and do what Jesus tells them. All the details get taken care of along the way—we just do not know how. In the process, says John, Jesus reveals his glory. I take this to mean that they got to see what he was really about, just a little bit—a glimpse of his truly remarkable identity. A little more epiphany, as it were.

I will confess here that I used to be somewhat puzzled by this story. I never had a problem believing that Jesus did it. I tend to have a simple understanding of Gospel stories about Jesus: I think they mean what they say. Also, since nothing is likely to be impossible for God in human form, I find it largely unnecessary and uninteresting to argue about whether this or that happened in the way that the story says it did. But I did have a problem understanding *why* he did it. Why this? Why start the most important ministry ever, early on in the most important story ever told, with some wine-making at a wedding? Really? In a world of wars and rumors of wars; of hurricanes and disasters and suffering, is this really the level at which Jesus chooses to engage with the human race?

But I have come to realize that John never tells us a story just because it happened. He is always interested in what it symbolized. Here the story of water into wine starts to make sense. The point seems to be that Jesus wants to take the life that we lead (symbolized by the jars of water for purification— a right and proper thing that played its appropriate part in lives of faithfulness to God) and fill it to overflowing with goodness and even joy. He takes our lives—water—and he turns them into new life—wine. Not just any wine, but the best. Lives that are full of flavor, full of intoxicating smells and tastes; in short, lives that are good to live, rich with experience. That is why Jesus' first sign, as it is called at the end of the story (verse 11), is turning water into wine. John wants to say that Jesus takes our daily life, and fills it with new life.

MARY TAKES HER SON TO A WEDDING... —JOHN 2

In due course, Jesus will address the problems, heartaches, struggles, and suffering. Indeed, he will take on the sins of the whole world; and there are many important things to say about the seriousness of that struggle between good and evil, not least of which is that—in the end—Jesus will win it, with life conquering death. But it is as if John is keen to say to us, "First, the good news! First you have to understand that all of that struggle and deliverance comes from a Jesus who wants us to experience new and life-affirming goodness." To put it most simply, Jesus invites us to a party. Who would not want to join in?

One church I know was asked recently to list some of its key characteristics. Many good and important factors made the list. One was tea and cake at the end of the Sunday service. A few people at the meeting where they were making the list thought this was not important enough to feature as one of their key characteristics. But tea and cake at the end of the service is not just a nice touch. It can be one important part of what life in the kingdom of God is about: celebrating the life-affirming goodness of all that Jesus offers us.

Of course, time spent together, even worshiping together, is not always happy, not always a party. It can be time to share experiences of difficulty and brokenness, of grief and loss. Even then, it is still a remarkable privilege to share such news together, to pray for one another, and to remember the presence of Jesus in the midst of broken-hearted worshipers, by taking bread and wine, recalling that our glimpse of the kingdom to come is still a glimpse from a darker and a harder place, even from the valley of the shadow of death. Even then, God still wants us to experience God's goodness.

Mary has a special place in Christian tradition, across the traditions. She was, as the early church concluded, the *theotokos*, the God-bearer. The argument was simple: if Christ was both truly God and truly human, indivisibly both, then Mary was not just the mother of Jesus the man, but she was the mother of God. When we think of it like this, what more significant role model for human response to Jesus could churches be looking for? Sadly, well-known disputes about how to express her precise role and significance end up clouding some churches' ability to benefit from the gospel witness to Mary. But her role in our story here in John 2 is in some ways a particularly powerful example of why we are well-advised to attend to her life and its witness. In passing, note that this is precisely why so many churches down through the centuries have celebrated the life and witness of specific "saints" from across the whole of the Christian story. At its root, such a practice is designed to recall that the saint being celebrated is pointing us to Jesus; or in other words, it is their Christian witness that is being celebrated.

Here Mary points us to Jesus as strongly as anyone ever does: "Do whatever he tells you." What Mary models here, as she does so often in her appearances in the Gospels, is a strange mixture of, on the one hand, not understanding what Jesus is doing, and on the other hand, insisting that whatever he is doing is the most important thing. That must have been a difficult balance for Mary to hold, as Jesus' mother: to have to admit that his ways were often difficult for her to understand, and that the way he speaks to her in this story does feel like the kind of way that a son can irritate a mother in seeming to think that he knows best. But if Mary manages to hold fast to focusing on what Jesus can

MARY TAKES HER SON TO A WEDDING . . . —JOHN 2

do, then by extension so can all of us who seek to learn from her example, indeed all of God's people.

The story of Jesus turning water into wine is a simple one, but it works on lots of different levels. At the end of the passage, Mary, the rest of Jesus' family, and the disciples follow Jesus on down to Capernaum and on into the rest of the story. It will not be an easy one for them, for Jesus, or (in very particular ways) for Mary. But as the church has known for two thousand years, Mary remains an extraordinary model for us in showing what it can mean to give her whole life to attending faithfully to whatever Jesus tells her, tells us, tells everyone, to do.

What does the future hold? Where is Jesus leading us and what is he going to do? We do not know. Is there much to worry about in the lives of our churches? Yes there is. Is there much to worry about in our own personal lives and the lives of those we know and love? Yes there is. Is there much to worry about in the world around us? Yes there is. Do we all have days when we want to pray, "Lord, we are in trouble, and we are out of ideas"? Yes we do.

But we hear this life-giving word from Mary: "Do whatever he tells you." We receive the goodness that he desires us to experience, whether it is as simple as wine at a wedding, or as complex as life in the midst of death. Our worries do not need to lead us to despair. Rather, like Mary, they might lead us to a complete and whole-hearted trust. Recall, as in our previous chapter, that it is when we are out of ideas, out of resources—and out of wine, in this case—that God says: now the real work can begin, as if God were to say, "Come to me and let me give you the overflowing wine of new life."

That is worth celebrating, week in and week out; in words of gospel life, or in bread and wine, or in music and prayer, or even in tea and cake. Week in and week out we attend to Mary's words, as she looked, puzzled but confident, at her wondrous Son: "Do whatever he tells you."

CHAPTER 4

True Love, or "What John 3:16 Really Means"—John 3

Read John 3:11–16 (and Numbers 21:4–9)

WHERE DO WE GET our picture of God?

We live in a world of so much stimulus, so much persuasion, so much manipulation of our senses, and in the face of all of that: where do we learn or receive our understanding of who God is?

For myself, when I was about six years old, I thought God was like Frank Bough. For the benefit of younger readers, or those who didn't have access to UK television in the 1970s, Frank Bough was the presenter of "Grandstand," the BBC's sports roundup program on a Saturday afternoon. Every week he would sit, relaxed and confident, brokering to that pre-Internet world the soccer scores. He looked (to my six-year-old eyes) incredibly old, centuries old—he must have been at least forty. I have reflected on *why* I thought God was like that, and I have concluded that it was because here was someone who knew the most important information in the world: the sports scores. Moreover, he could be relied on every week to tell us this information, obtaining it from the farthest ends of the universe, exotic places far away across England

33

like Sheffield or Exeter, which were in themselves complete mysteries to me. This was omniscience and omnipotence all rolled into one, if ever I saw it. Of course, on reflection, saying such a thing is just to decide what God must be like in theory, and then to look for a candidate to fill that description. (Just to be sure that there is no possibility of misunderstanding here: I no longer believe that God is anything like Frank Bough, for reasons to do with both God and Frank Bough.) But might it be the case that our own image of God comes from sources that are in their own way equally bizarre?

Christians are invited to affirm, very simply, that one key source for our picture of God is Jesus; and the place where we find Jesus teaching us how to understand God is in the Gospels; and that one of the most important things Jesus wants to tell us about God is that God is a loving God. That this is hardly a new insight does not mean we should not pause and reflect on it.

I am inclined to think, for example, that this point is key to the Gospel of John. If our picture of God is not of a loving God, then we have probably been getting it from somewhere else. John will not put it quite as bluntly as this until the book of 1 John: "God is love" (1 John 4:8). In chapter 3 of John's Gospel, there is a verse even more famous than that: we have arrived indeed at John 3:16: "For God so loved the world that he gave his only Son, so that everyone who believes in him may not perish, but may have eternal life." That is good news. As mentioned at the beginning of this book, the word for "good news" in Christian theology is "gospel," which is also the word from which we get the adjective "evangelical," meaning "of the gospel," "relating to the gospel," or "gospel-shaped." So here we are in John 3, and surely that is reason enough for a gospel-shaped reflection; an evangelical reading—of John 3:16 no less.

One might think that that would be fairly straightforward. Here is the reader—let me introduce you to the good news. Good news, let me introduce you to the reader; go off and enjoy each other's company; we all live happily ever after, or to quote the verse, "that we may not perish but have eternal life." Is it not as simple as that?

I think John's understanding of why we find this good news hard to tune into is because the claim that God is a loving God is not a freestanding piece of information, on a level playing field, to which we are invited to give our assent after calculating all our options. John 3:16, to be specific, is not an isolated fact that we are supposed to learn and add to our store of understanding, and thus just tick off as another piece of information in the world in which we live.

It is more like an argument, in the midst of competing counterarguments, compelling counterclaims, stories that try to crowd out our story. Our story is the story of God the creator, who made the earth and all that is in it, and who *loved us so much* that even when we showed very little love in return, the creator God still sent the Son, Jesus, so that we might believe in him, and not perish, but have eternal life.

Now notice how John positions this famous verse. He does not start with it. Interestingly, many people through the centuries since seem to have thought that you can start with it. They seem to have thought that if you quote John 3:16, just like that, it is supposed to make sense, and there is your picture of God, a loving God, and that is that. Of course this is not so much *wrong*, as a bit naive about how likely we are to understand it, or understand what is at stake. Instead, John backtracks and takes a run up at this kind of claim, by starting his story, as we saw earlier, back in chapter 1, with "In the beginning . . ." That was a bit like saying that whatever other stories we may have heard, this one outflanks them all. This one is a bigger story, and one that makes better sense of the same confusing world that everyone else is also trying to understand and work out. We need that big picture to see how all the little bits of John's story hang together.

This brings us to the heart of how John is trying to tell us about Jesus, who is trying to tell us about God: that God is a God of love, and that what this love looks like is shown in Jesus' words, and his actions, and his life, and his death, and his being raised again.

We do not get to define love in our own way and then ask whether God matches up to it. That is not how we work out who God really is. According to the Hollywood story, we should imagine beautiful music, the radiant dying of the light; he looks at her, she looks at him, and he realizes that of course he should abandon his job and the life he has been struggling to maintain and go backpacking with her across the Alps; she realizes, as the sun sets across the Seine, that Paris is where she is truly supposed to be, and this moment is supposed to trump her plans to fly back home and go to law school. How can the love of God compete with these romantic fantasies? Because with God, we do not, and we will not always have Paris; rather, we will always have Golgotha, the place of the cross. The kind of love upon which we are invited to fasten is a love that is determined to hold on in there, in the face of death and despair, and never ever give up, to find that (who would have thought?) life, liberty, and the pursuit of happiness take you through the heart of

TRUE LOVE, OR "WHAT JOHN 3:16 REALLY MEANS"—JOHN 3

darkness itself, and then out the other side into resurrection life, eternal life, new life.

I want to say two things about love, or in particular God's love. One is about the link between God's love and our knowledge of who God is. The other is about what John 3:16 is really saying once you see it as part of this bigger picture. I hope that both of these points will be good news.

First, then, love and knowledge (I know that sounds a bit abstract, but bear with me). There is a great verse back in 1 John again that makes this link: "We know love by this, that he [Jesus] laid down his life for us." (Oddly enough, this verse is also chapter 3, verse 16, but in 1 John instead.) God defines love for us, and defines it by pointing us to Jesus. But actually the same argument is at work here in the Gospel of John, chapter 3. In John 3:11, we have Jesus saying "Very truly, I tell you, we speak of what we know." That is Jesus pointing out that he is uniquely in a position to tell us what is truly going on with God because, as verse 13 puts it, he has been there, with God, up above, or "in the beginning" (back to John 1:1 again). Hence Jesus alone can truly reveal God to us.

Actually, the way John works through this chapter is rather interesting. He starts with a story about Nicodemus, a Pharisee, who comes to Jesus by night to ask him some questions. This story functions a bit like an illustration of the point John is trying to make. For ten verses, John has them arguing back and forth, about being born anew, born from above, born again, born a second time, born of water and Spirit, and Nicodemus, who seems to be a decent sort of man, keeps defaulting back to "Well, this makes no sense, I don't follow . . . I mean, entering back into the womb, and all that." As Jesus reminds him, he—Nicodemus—is supposed to be the teacher, but he cannot even explain where the wind is blowing from. That may seem a rather random point, except that perhaps it helps to know that the word for "wind" and the word for "spirit" are the same (*pneuma*). Jesus wraps up the story along the lines of "You're not really on top of all this, are you, Nic. You may have a very respectable teaching ministry, and a nice line in *pneuma* resources, but you just don't get it, do you?"

Then, in verse 11, John suddenly seems to cut the illustration, and Jesus starts addressing "you" plural: "You do not receive our testimony," as if now he is addressing us, you and me, the readers of the Gospel, as we are fought over, backwards and forwards, by the stories that fly around our world, by the different testimonies to truth, the different claims being made, and the different tales being told. So how are we supposed to know what to make of it all?

The Nicodemus story seems to serve as a kind of illustration of how it is possible to get caught up in the puzzles—the fascinating puzzles, admittedly—of understanding God and God's ways, and trying to sort out the things we do and do not know about God, but missing the core thing that makes sense of everything else: that God loves us. John's claim here, bluntly, is that we know the truth by receiving God's love. I wonder if John would even say that it may not be possible to picture God as a God of love on our own terms. In other words: to *see* that God is a loving God requires us to *receive* God's own enactment of what love really is, found in Jesus. Not Paris, but Golgotha. Not the endless attempt to fit God into our understanding, but the love of God revealed in the life and death, the cross and resurrection, of Christ. He is not a fair-weather God who is good for those days when we can tell which way the wind is blowing, but a God who will stick with us through thick and through thin, and who says that he will wait, until the end of the world, if that is how long it takes.

This brings us at last to John 3:16. "For God so loved the world that he gave his only Son, so that everyone who believes in him may not perish but may have eternal life."

God's love navigates a tricky middle path between two very widely held pictures of God in our world today. On the one hand, God is a cruel judge, a kind of vindictive and arbitrary figure who wants some people to go to heaven and some people to go to hell. The people who believe this include many outside the church who think it is a good enough reason to give up on God, as well as many inside the church who are laboring under a serious misunderstanding of what is going on in Scripture. Then, on the other hand, God is Santa Claus, a God whose notion of love is precisely the warm and fuzzy one we have talked about, and whose sole role in the cosmos is to be . . . nice, and whenever life is not nice, this is somehow a breakdown in God's insurance coverage. This is also a view widely held outside the church, in fact sometimes viewed quite positively outside the church, but again quite popular inside it, where we stand to sing "It's a Nice World After All" in the key of Disney.

But according to John 3:16, God's love involves loving the world. What we need to know here is that this word, "world," is largely a negative word in John's Gospel. The world is the place of darkness, of night, of disbelief. It is humanity understood as set against God. It is nothing to do with our environment, the world being an ecosystem that we must love and look after, which may be a perfectly fine message to take from the Bible as a whole, but it is not what John is talking about here. This is God loving humankind in the face of all the ways that humankind denies or turns against God. That is why John says "God *so* loved the world": what is remarkable is that God would love it at all, given how hostile it is to God.

This is important because, as we said at the beginning, John 3:16 is not just some isolated fact about how much God loves us. Rather, it is an argument in the midst of a battle between good and evil, or light and darkness. The love that God has here is remarkable. It is love during wartime. It is an act of reaching out across fundamental opposition and offering life to everyone. That brings us to the next word worth noticing in this verse: "everyone." It is not a limited offer. The good news is available precisely to those who are classified as part of this "world": those who are against God.

This glorious truth, worth celebrating always and forever, should surely have been a simple cause for rejoicing. However, I feel compelled to suggest that there are those who have lost the plot here because they have become tangled up in questions designed to understand this loving initiative of God, but that have not helped. Instead, their questions have turned it into a complicated and quite disturbing image of a God who delights in saving some and dismissing others. The problem lies partly in trying to isolate parts of the story in order to interrogate them with abstract questions about things like "free will" and "predestination," or asking "if God is sovereign, then how can God be loving and not save everyone?" You know the kind of thing. You may even have wondered this yourself. So, with some misgivings, I think a brief reflection on this issue may be called for here, always acknowledging that there are other ways of looking at it, but this is the way that makes sense to me.

God is sovereign—this is not negotiable. But the image of "sovereign" means exactly what it says when it is used in Scripture—we might think of prayers to the "Sovereign Lord" in Acts 4:24 or Revelation 6:10, for example. It means that God rules, or reigns. The New Testament phrase for the "rule" or "reign" of God is in fact "the kingdom of God." It means that the world we live in, despite appearances, really does belong to God, who is the king of this kingdom, or as the New Testament puts it at one point, the king of kings (1 Tim 6:15). The way some people talk about "free will" makes it sound like they envisage it as an alternative to God's sovereignty, but I really do believe that that is a muddled view. The alternative to God being king is not that the world becomes a neutral place where we can make free and informed decisions about love and war. According to Scripture, the alternative is that the world is a place where our will is corrupted, struggling under the onslaught of sin (or "sin, death, and the devil," as the traditional language has put it); where we would in fact have no real freedom at all. Thus it is precisely *because* God is king—or because of the sovereignty of God, in other words—that we have *any* chance to exercise our will. Far from divine sovereignty and human freedom being a zero sum game, where the more of one you have, the less of the other you have, it is only because God is sovereign—the king of the kingdom—that we have the chance to exercise any kind of freedom at all.

So, to come back to John chapter 3, God's love—which is like a rescue mission in the face of adversity—should be understood as aiming to rescue everybody. It is, however, a love that is entering into an ongoing conflict in which humans manage to demonstrate over and again that they might still choose darkness over the light. We should take note of John 3:17 too: God did not send Jesus to condemn the world, but to save everyone. And yet, in verse 18, a certain kind of judgment follows if you then choose to turn away from this offer, because you were already implicated in this conflict. Remember, there is no neutral option.

While we are pondering these things in our hearts, this may be the occasion to clarify that when we talk of God's judgment, we are talking about the distinction between what is life-giving and what is not. God's judgment is fundamentally about justice and holding open the door to life; that everyone, according to John 3:16, might come on board. But again, "judgment" is another term about which there has been a concerted disinformation campaign, worthy of Screwtape, trying to get us to imagine that we are all so much more civilized than needing to believe in a God who judges. As if judging were some kind of horrific imposition on daily life, like getting voted off of the "X-Factor" after using a gospel choir to sing backing for a version of Leonard Cohen's "Hallelujah." What a completely confused world we live in.

Without judgment, there is no justice. Everyone who has ever been treated badly knows that. The only people who dislike judgment are the ones who are doing rather nicely in the present system, thank you very much, and would rather it was not disrupted. People at the bottom of the ladder, on the other hand, are desperate for a God who will step in and judge. At heart, Jesus' judgments are designed to bring life, in all sorts of generous and unmerited ways.

TRUE LOVE, OR "WHAT JOHN 3:16 REALLY MEANS"—JOHN 3

Finally, very briefly, let us consider eternal life (with a nod to the irony of considering eternal life very briefly). In John 3:16, the phrase "eternal life" does not—at least primarily—refer to living forever, as if all the hope for a loved future is delayed to the everlasting resurrection life to come. It is a phrase that means something like "the life of the age to come," and it is about the *kind* of life that God wants for us, rather than just its duration. Eternal life, in John's Gospel, is about experiencing God as the king of God's kingdom even now. God loves us so much—God *so* loves us—that we might even experience light in the midst of the darkness, right now.

Along the way, John refers us to an Old Testament passage from the book of Numbers (21:4–9) where Moses lifted up the snake on the pole so that whoever, in the midst of the wilderness, was suffering could be healed right where they were. That is the image John appropriates to describe Jesus being "lifted up" on the cross (John 3:14). You can receive life, right where you are, even though where you are may remain—at least for now—something of a wilderness.

The image of God we get from the Gospel of John is an image of a God whose sovereign judgments work for our good. God's involvement in our world brings us life, even now, on this side of the resurrection, so remarkable is the gift of life that God is offering us. The next time someone tries to bombard you with a counter-testimony, a more suspicious story, to trouble your soul or to persuade you either that God is nasty or that God is merely nice, I invite you to recall this better story, which is the Gospel according to John, and which is good news. Or, if you cannot recollect the whole book, remember this one verse: For God so loved the world that he gave his only Son, so that everyone who believes in him may not perish but may have eternal life. This is the word of the Lord, meant to carry us through every trial or temptation that may come upon us, today, tomorrow, and always. Thanks be to God.

CHAPTER 5

Encounter at the Well—John 4

Read John 4:5–42 (and Exodus 17:1–7)

ONCE UPON A TIME, a man sat down by a well to draw water; along came a woman, and they fell into conversation. That is the setup for this story, but whose story is it?

Possibility 1: Jacob. He meets Rachel as she tends her father's sheep (Gen 29). They fall in love, and off they go, and although it takes a few years to sort it out, it ends up happily ever after.

Possibility 2: Moses. He's on the run from a bit of trouble in Egypt, and he meets Zipporah, daughter of the priest of Midian (Exod 2). They fall in love, and off they go, happily ever after.

Possibility 3: Jesus. He's sat at Jacob's well in the heat of the day, by the cool of the pool. Along comes a Samaritan woman (John 4). Will they fall in love? Will it be happy ever after? The answer to these questions is "yes," but not in the way you think.

It turns out that this woman has had five husbands, and the man she is now living with is not her husband (v. 18). That is six men already, and she has not yet found her true love. Who will be number seven, the perfect number, the one to bring to an end this restless searching for a man in her life? It is a New Testament question. The answer is Jesus.

To say that she falls in love with him is not to say that this is a romantic encounter. It is not. Despite occasional sensationalist attempts to say otherwise, Jesus never married, never had a romantic relationship that we know of, and remained single for all his short time on this earth. Yet in the process of this story, does John not say to us that it is indeed possible to love him with our whole hearts, our whole minds, our whole selves? That to spend our lives following God is, in this sense, to love Jesus—to have Jesus be the one who fulfills our deepest needs?

The way John expresses this in chapter 4 is with some well-known language: Jesus is the living water, and if we come to the living water, then we will not be thirsty again. The woman in the story represents us. She responds to the point about water by saying, "But sir, you have no bucket, and the well is deep." That can sound uneasily like us: God offers us life in all its fullness, and we immediately jump to practical problems: Yes, but we are thirsty! Thanks for the eternal life and forgiveness and love and all that, but someone has to service the boiler and give out the invitations to the coffee morning and clean and cook and sort and arrange. If God is going to give us living water, well obviously the first thing we are going to have to do is set up a committee to buy some suitable pots to keep this water in. What use is a gift of living water if we do not have the right vessels to store it in?

To which I imagine Jesus says, "This is not about buckets and wells. The right vessels for this living water are you yourselves, women and men of God, the living stones out of whom God's church is made." After all, recall the Old

Testament passage in which Moses provided water for the Israelites in the wilderness by striking the rock, which then emitted water (Exod 17:1-7). Who would have thought that God would take care of mass thirst by using a convenient local rock? And if God can do that, then the shortage of a bucket or two is not going to stand in his way in John 4, as Jesus talks to the woman, sat by the well.

The woman thinks she wants this living water (v. 15). "Sir, give me this water, so that I may never be thirsty or have to keep coming here to draw water." (Possible subtext: and thus I could avoid having to talk to strange people like you.)

Jesus says, "Go, call your husband and come back." Now, why did he do that? The conversation was going well. He had got her to ask for the gift of living water, though she had not asked for it in those words, but still she seemed genuinely interested. Clearly her backstory with men was complicated. So why did Jesus have to be so socially awkward and put his finger on this highly sensitive personal matter: Husband? What husband? Either forlornly or stubbornly, she replies, "I have no husband." But not—it becomes apparent—for lack of trying. She is on to her sixth man. But here she is, back at the well, seeking water, not satisfied.

So I wonder. Did Jesus know that she was trying to find her fulfillment in having a husband, and that it was not working out for her? I say this carefully, and with the permission of my wife, but I think this is important to say in our world of movie blockbuster happy endings where everything seems to be about having the perfect partner: a husband—or a wife—is not the one golden key to living a fulfilled life. A good marriage is a wonderful blessing, there is no doubt about that. But on its own, a marriage cannot bear all the weight of making two people happy ever after. At least, according to John chapter 4, because as well as any friendships, relationships, or marriage partners that we may have, we also need Jesus; whose gift of life, of living water, never runs out. Only Jesus can meet our neverending needs . . . for water, and then also in turn for acceptance, for love, for forgiveness.

After the talk about her husbands, the woman sort of gets the point, by saying "Sir, I see that you are a prophet," but she makes one last attempt to block out the implications, and move the conversation on to what prophets think about this and that, and still Jesus keeps pressing, talking about worship and spirit and truth, until she says, perhaps a bit nervously now: "Well anyway, I mustn't keep you [I am paraphrasing; we usually say "I mustn't keep you" when we are wanting to get away ourselves]. They say the Messiah is on his way, and I'm sure he will sort it all out." I imagine her trying to fill her water jar and get away before this strange man asks any more uncomfortable questions. Her last words are hanging in the air, about the Messiah, and he reaches out (we may imagine), and touches her arm as she turns to go, and says "I am He." In other words, "The Messiah—that's me. The one who is speaking to you."

The disciples return at just this point, and find Jesus alone and talking to a woman, which could turn out to be scandalous in its time. She, on the other hand, has just heard the most remarkable thing she has ever heard in her life, and you have to recognize that she has heard five men tell her they will love her forever, and none of them turned out to be right, so she has heard some pretty remarkable things. But now this is the most remarkable thing of all. The man she is talking to is the Messiah, and she just has to tell everyone about that.

What does he mean when he says "the Messiah"? The word comes from an Old Testament term meaning an "anointed one." It is used at the time of Jesus to refer to the one who would fulfill God's rescue plan for his people: lead them out of darkness into light, and deal with their sins. To be the Messiah was to be the promised one who would bring life out of death, and light out of darkness, and Jesus says, "I am He."

The rest of the story sees her running off to gather people around to hear about this extraordinary encounter, and come and meet this man. Today she is talking to you and me, two thousand years later. Many Samaritans came to believe because of her testimony. How many people in the twenty-first century might come to believe because of her testimony, which points us to the man who says "God is Spirit, and those who worship him must worship in spirit and truth." By the time John's Gospel ends, we will have learned that the messiah, Jesus, is one with the Father and the Spirit. We are meeting God in human form, waiting for us by the well, and we are invited to fall in love with him.

Quite an invitation. Where will it lead us? Two observations. First: it is hard to fall in love with someone you never listen to. So if we want to experience this living water, this water that will leave us never thirsty again, then we need to hear the words of life that Jesus offers us. There is a simple way to do this that we need to take seriously. We need to read the Gospels. Matthew, Mark, Luke, and John allow us to meet Jesus—they allow us to be right there with ordinary people like the Samaritan woman as they meet with Jesus, and we can hear him talking. We should not overlook this basic way of meeting with Jesus and listening to him.

Secondly, it is hard to love someone you never talk to. So we have to talk to Jesus. The traditional language for this, of course, is prayer. Here is my suggestion about prayer, particularly relevant for all those among us who ever find ourselves drinking a glass of water. Why not say this simple prayer every time you get yourself a drink of water in the next few days: "Jesus, thank you that you are our living water." You can say the same if you are using water to make a cup of tea or coffee. Talking to Jesus can be as simple as that. Arguably, it *should* be as simple as that.

Those are my two observations about what it means for us to fall in love with Jesus. Listen to him—read our Bibles—and talk to him—pray. May we keep our eyes focused on the one who says "I am He—come to me and you will never be thirsty again."

CHAPTER 6

Walking on the Water of the New Creation—John 6

Read John 6:16–24 (and Exodus 13:17–18 and 14:21–29)

OLD MAN JOHN WRITES his Gospel: in chapter 6, Jesus walks on the water. John has had a long time to think about it, and this is what he says.

First, something happened. John remembers it. Jesus fed five thousand people with five loaves and two fishes. Then, that night, there was a boat, a storm, a list of who had got on and who had not, and a count of how many boats had departed. Jesus was not among those who boarded the boat. However, the next morning, he was with those who disembarked. They said they saw him on the water. They were afraid. He said, "Do not be afraid." So let us say that that is what happened. Jesus walked on the water.

And yet, thinks John, this is not the whole story—or rather, this is only the surface of the story, and Matthew and Mark have both already told that, so what was really going on?

Secondly, then, something significant happened. A sign, if you will. As with everything he writes, Old Man John

51

writes it very carefully, masking deep wisdom, refracting the glory of the gospel of God through the telling of stories about Jesus traveling over land and (in this particular case) sea. Slow down, says John. Still your frantic searching; your speed reading; your restless activity; your desire to master each day God gives you. Slow down, and listen, for we have words of eternal life.

Verse 17b, somewhere in the region of "It was now dark and Jesus had not yet come to them," or whatever bland statement of scene-setting our late modern translations reduce this to. Let's render it a bit differently: *"and darkness had already come, but not yet come to them was Jesus."* It took John years to write it. The least we could do is take a few moments to read it.

The darkness of which John speaks (by and large it is only John in the New Testament who ever speaks of this darkness) is the same darkness we had back in the beginning: John 1:5, where we recall that the apostle of poetry and prophecy wrote, so memorably, "The light shines in the darkness and the darkness has not overcome it." This darkness, which haunts our world, then as now—this is the darkness that had already come. But *not yet come*—that would be Jesus. We are between the times. Will the darkness win? The answer to this question turns out to be "no."

John will go on to say that Jesus is the light of the world, so that we do not have to walk in darkness. When the hour comes for Jesus to turn towards his death, it is his last opportunity to tell us that we walk in light instead. Then when Judas breaks bread with him, takes his bread and slips away, all John will say (in John 13:30) is: "And it was night." When it is dark in John's Gospel, he does not just mean that the sun has gone down. He means that hope is fighting for its life.

So darkness had already come, but not Jesus. Then there he is: three or four miles out, in the midst of the storm, walking on the sea. John, what does this mean? He adds two profound details, sharpening his quill, letting each word do real work. One: in response to the disciples' fear, Jesus says, "It is I." Except what he actually says is "I am," which is ungrammatical but oh-so-significant, for those with ears to hear, who remember the God of Moses: "I am who I am/I am has sent you" (Exod 3:14). Two: on taking him into the boat, John writes that the boat "came immediately to the land to which they were going."

John's work is done here. He needs to get back to explaining the significance of the feeding of the five thousand, which will now fall into place. But the walking on the water, so elegantly handled, so briefly described—just what happened here? About mystery he was never wrong, old Master John, how well he understood. With tears in his eyes, he submits to brutal paraphrase: yes, he says, Jesus is the great I am, who comes to us in the darkness and leads us across the sea to our own promised land. But gospel truth is not built to move like that, blundering and blunt, in plain sight. It catches you in the boat of your own turmoil, on the high seas of your own despair, amidst the darkness that never ever wins in the end.

Let me put it in context. By that I mean let us go back to Genesis and reread in the light of what Jesus does here. In the beginning—an opening that John himself borrowed, if you recall—darkness was over the deep, and the wind or breath or spirit (the *ruach*) of God hovered over the waters. Or, in

53

other words, it was already dark, but Jesus had not yet come. But God separated the waters and made dry land appear; and there was evening, and there was morning, and all that was on the third day (if such a detail could be significant). Then in the Exodus, that same *ruach*, meaning "wind" or "spirit," of God blew across the waters, which divided, and dry land opened up before them. On this dry land, God led the Israelites across the sea to the promised land, on a night of storms and turmoil, of darkness and danger and despair

> *Rejoice, heavenly powers! Sing, choirs of angels!*
>
> *Exult, all creation around God's throne! . . .*
>
> *This is the night when first you saved our fathers:*
>
> *you freed the people of Israel from their slavery*
>
> *and led them dry-shod through the sea.*
>
> *This is the night when the pillar of fire destroyed the darkness of sin.*[1]

That is the story John is telling, although he is telling it about Jesus, so that in the end it will prove irresistible to proclaim:

> *This is the night when Jesus Christ*
>
> *broke the chains of death*
>
> *and rose triumphant from the grave.*

But right now, John is waiting for the other shoe to drop. There is something different about this picture. Which piece of the story in John 6 so conspicuously converts the Exodus

---

1. This is one translation of parts of the "*Exsultet*," the Easter proclamation traditionally sung by a deacon at dawn on Easter morning, and thought to have been written sometime between the fifth and the eighth centuries.

story so that it becomes a "new exodus" story? It is the difference between walking through the water on dry land, and walking *on* the water. Jesus does not need the Spirit of God to prepare the path for him, because he himself is Lord of all creation, and anticipates for us the walk to the land, the world, that is to come, the promised new creation. Behold, he makes all things new.

John settles himself down to write again. What follows the exodus? The manna in the wilderness, of course. What follows the new exodus? Jesus, the bread of life himself.

How often do we, at the end of a long day, reflect on that sense of weariness that comes upon us as we gaze, perhaps idly, out of the window and note that it has already grown dark. But the long day and the wearinesss may not fundamentally be statements about the hour on the clock, but about the world in which we live. If we are tired, maybe it is not because we are busy (though we may well be), but because we live in a fallen world. If we are overwhelmed, maybe it is not because our workload is heavy, or our context is unsettling, or our friendships are complicated (though all these things may be true), but because our world is witnessing the conflict of light and darkness, of good and evil, to which John's Gospel testifies. In short, the problems that tend to preoccupy us are evidence of a greater problem, which is that sin and evil are afoot. We are not going to turn the world around by trying harder, singing louder, or strategizing better.

We come to the heart of the matter, as Old Man John paints it for us in his Gospel. It is this: The world is broken, and you cannot fix it. And your hearts will be broken, if they are not broken already, and you cannot fix them either. This would be an impossible burden for us to bear, were it not that there is someone who bears it for us, who—uniquely—does not sink down below the waves, as creation gives way in birth pains to the new creation.

Lord we are afraid, and with good reason. But he says to us, "I am—it is I—do not be afraid." The darkness seems to overwhelm us. But he says, "By no means, the light shines in the darkness, and the darkness will not overcome it." Lord, really? Even in the face of death, the final enemy? But he says, "I am the resurrection and the life, and all shall be gathered together on that far shore, in the land to which we are going. So as often as you remember this, eat the bread, and drink the wine, which are given for the healing of the world."

To recap, we first said that something happened. Jesus walked on the water. Secondly, John wrote about it, full of grace and truth. Thirdly, then, if we have ears to hear, this is how John did it:

> When evening came, his disciples went down to the sea, got into a boat, and started across the sea to Capernaum. It was now dark, and Jesus had not yet come to them. The sea became rough because a strong wind was blowing. When they had rowed about three or four miles, they saw Jesus walking on the sea and coming near the boat, and they were terrified. But he said to them, "I am; do not be afraid." Then they wanted to take him into the boat, and immediately the boat reached the land toward which they were going.

On so many levels, this is the word of the Lord, so thanks be to God.

CHAPTER 7

Not Dead Yet—John 11

Read John 11:1–45 (and Ezekiel 37)

I AM GOING TO cheat—or at least, I will take a roundabout approach to John 11. As we have said more than once, we need the Old Testament to help us read the New Testament well. So, in turning to John 11 and focusing on the death of Lazarus, we are going to go by way of Ezekiel 37. In fact, the death and resurrection of Lazarus is almost certainly incorporated by John in order to draw us into thinking about the death and resurrection of Jesus. That is our real focus: the death of Jesus, never to be considered in isolation from the resurrection of Jesus. They are two sides of the same coin—no death without resurrection, no resurrection without death. To those lost in gloominess and overwhelmed by failure, I want to say that there is a resurrection! To those unwilling to face the realities of life and be realistic about difficulties, I want to say, first there is the death. It is a kind of balancing act in our faith, between defeat and victory, but there is one really important sense—we shall realize—in which it is not an equal balancing act or a fair match between death and resurrection.

First comes Ezekiel. Now, I have some sympathy with those who find it hard going to ever encounter the words "First—Ezekiel." Who knows anything about this bizarre prophet? What does this have to do with us? Although this is not the occasion to go into great detail about this unusual figure and his unusual book, I do want to spend just long enough with him to get the right ideas in view for our reading of John. In the process, I hope too that we might catch some glimpse of the wonderful world of the Old Testament, even if only briefly.

Here is what you need to know to hear this prophet well. First, he is prophesying in Judah (that's the old southern kingdom) around the beginning of the sixth century BCE. One of the first things he sees, more or less, is a vision of the glory of the Lord departing from the temple. It rather sounds like he is watching it fly away on the ancient version of a helicopter, but that is for another day. Why is the glory of the Lord departing from the temple, and what does that mean? It means that God has run out of patience with the people of Israel and is about to abandon them to being exiled.

In 586 BCE (give or take) the Babylonians arrive and take Israel away into captivity. For thirty-three chapters, Ezekiel has been trying to warn them that this is going to happen, and has been patiently pointing out to them that it is all very well being self-justifying and saying "God is good" so all will be well, but if you do not recognize that you have rejected God's will, then you are going to be in trouble. Then in chapter 33, around verse 21, someone makes it out of the chaos of Jerusalem, finds their way out to Ezekiel, who is mainly based in Babylon himself, and tells him that "The city has fallen." It has actually happened. Nebuchadnezzar had triggered his own version of Brexit's famous "Article 50," and Israel was on its way out into exile. Its leaders were deported; its temple worship stuttered to a halt; and the land lay, not exactly empty, but chaotic and full of despair, to be ruled over by what we might choose to call BKIP: the Babylonian King Independence Party.

This is the background to the vision that we find in Ezekiel 37, probably the one famous passage in the whole book: the valley of dry bones. The only part of Ezekiel to lend itself to a popular spiritual song—number 371 in *Hymns Very Ancient and Modern*, in three parts for choir, soloist, and organ—is "Dem Bones, Dem Bones, Dem Dry Bones." All together now: "The knee bone's connected to the thigh bone. The thigh bone's connected to the hip bone. The hip bone's connected to the . . . Now hear the word of the Lord!" All of this comes straight from Ezekiel, although arguably misses something of the prophet's point and drifts into being one of those strangest of musical items: Bible songs about body parts—"Father Abraham had many sons, many sons had Father Abraham . . . right arm! left arm!"—which does not get us very far with the book of Genesis either. (Some suggest that this may be because it was written originally in honor of Abraham Lincoln.)

In any case, in Ezekiel 37:1, the prophet is picked up and carried away in a vision ("by the Spirit," he says) and set down in a valley full of bones. We are told explicitly by the end that these bones represent the whole house of Israel; which is not a very subtle image. It is basically saying that Israel, in its scattered and distressed state, is dead. It has no life. It is just a pile of bones. In verse 2, the bones are everywhere, and they are very dry. (As per the song, you will recall.)

The Lord says, "These bones... these bones... are gonna walk around." Well not quite. What he actually says is that Ezekiel should prophesy to these dry bones, and say to them, "Hear the word of the Lord!... I will cause breath to enter you and you shall live." The word for breath here is *ruach* (which we encountered when we were considering John 6, and is one of the rare Hebrew words that it may be worth our while learning). As noted previously, it means "breath," "wind," or "spirit" (or all three), and it is everywhere in this passage, just like it is everywhere in creation: back in Genesis 1, the *ruach* of God hovers over the waters; in Exodus, the *ruach* of God blows across the sea to make dry land appear and lead the people out to freedom; and here, in Ezekiel 37, the *ruach* of God is breathed into the bones, similar to the way that God breathed life into the original dust of the earth to make Adam. God brings the life of the spirit (*ruach* again) into the bones, and the four winds blow (that's four *ruach*s once more, believe it or not), and from all the corners of the earth comes this life-giving power or wind/breath/spirit of God, and the bones are built up into a living and breathing army.

In case the image is not strong enough for us, God explains it in a further image to Ezekiel: "I am going to bring you up from your graves, O my people," and bring them back to the land of Israel. He will put within them his spirit, which is (you guessed it) *ruach* again.

Right here, in the middle of this Old Testament prophetic book, we have one of the Bible's most powerful pictures of resurrection: not just individual resurrection, but all of God's people, raised out of dry death and brought back to spirit-filled life. In 585 BCE, roughly, in the aftermath of exile, when all seemed lost and it would have been so easy to say "God has forgotten us," comes this magnificent promise of return from exile to the home land, a return from death to new life, restoration in the power of God's spirit.

There are thirty-two chapters of worry and judgment and impending disaster, but once the disaster has happened, and all is lost, then God acts in power to bring new life. You cannot have resurrection if you are not dead first. As the New Testament puts it, the old way of life has to die so that new life can enter in. I wonder if the church in some parts of the West in the twenty-first century has really understood this?

Now imagine that we know our Old Testaments, and that all this is in our minds as we turn to John and encounter the story of Lazarus in John 11. This is a wonderful story about the turmoil of emotions that are being experienced by Mary and Martha, and in the end by Jesus himself. It famously includes the shortest verse in the King James translation of the Bible—John 11:35, "Jesus wept." (The NRSV translation waffles around this a bit, and turns it into "Jesus began to weep," but most translations even today just go for "Jesus wept.") He is weeping because he is at the tomb where Lazarus died. Yet the odd thing is that he is about to raise him with his thunderous cry of "Lazarus come out!" so that (in my opinion), in one of the most startlingly understated moments of the whole Bible, we read, "The dead man came out." (For understatement it can perhaps only be compared to the King James translation of 2 Kings 19:35, where the Assyrian army has been slaughtered, and the translation reads, in its wonderfully misjudged way, "and when they arose early in the morning, behold they were all dead corpses.")

I have to say, I was always a bit puzzled by this incident at the grave of Lazarus. Jesus is about to raise him back to life, but he stands there for a moment before the tomb and he weeps. Clearly this is not, at least straightforwardly, a story of a happy ending pure and simple. Jesus does not turn up and say "It's ok, I'm here, and all shall be well," even though, in one sense, it is. But he weeps—presumably because even though he is about to ensure that life triumphs over death in this particular instance, he is distraught because he sees before him the evidence that death is wreaking its havoc in our world. Mary and Martha have lost a brother. People's lives have been overturned. Lazarus is dead, and therefore we weep—even though Jesus knows that this is not the final word.

Death wreaks havoc in our world, and it breaks our hearts; just like sin and evil wreak havoc in our world and break God's heart. Our lives are reduced to dry bones, and we so easily lose our hope; our belief in a God who is bigger than these enemies. But knowing that God is bigger does not take away the pain. Jesus wept. When in the presence of death, we acknowledge the brokenness of God's good creation.

Now we come to the point I started to make at the beginning, about the imbalance between death and life; or between death and resurrection. When Lazarus is raised back to life in John 11, it is undoubtedly a wondrous and joyful thing, but it is precisely a raising *back to life*, and in due course, Lazarus will grow old and will die again. He has come back from death, back to life, and he will die again.

What Ezekiel imagined seems to be even more remarkable than this kind of coming back to life. We may perhaps understand what Ezekiel imagined as a full-bodied resurrection—literally bodies full of new life and energy—of a kind that even Lazarus did not experience. But Jesus did. So, in the sense just carefully spelled out, I do not think Jesus came back to life, at the end of the Gospel, and I do not think that that is what the church celebrates at Easter. He did not enter into death and then back out, back into this life. Rather, he went right into the heart of death, experienced it fully, surrendered to it, and then went on, and came through and out the other side, into new resurrection life, raised up by the life-giving power of God's spirit, his *ruach*. Jesus' resurrection body is not his old body restored. It is a new thing, a strange and wondrous thing, capable of entering locked rooms, passing through doors, not because he is a ghost and can drift through physical barriers, but rather because he has turned the whole world upside down, and in fact his resurrection body is *more physically real* than our tired old three-dimensional created world, so that not even walls and locked doors can hold him. Oh yes, and he needs food. Fish, mainly, it would seem. If you want a head start on the resurrection life, eat fish. You read it here first.

But the big point is this: resurrection life is not the cancelling out of death, but the complete triumphing over death that swallows up our experiences of defeat and despair and dismay. It is not a fair fight. Death and resurrection are not equally matched. Resurrection wins in the end.

But until that day, like Jesus, we may weep in the presence of death, struggle against the forces of darkness in our lives, just like Israel in exile, or Mary and Martha before the grave of their brother, and we await the life-transforming *ruach* (the wind-breath-spirit) of God come to set us free. Just when everything seems lost, God wins. When we are at our most burdened, we turn to the one who bears our burdens for us. When we are broken, God makes us whole.

In a low-level way, we may think of it like this: The next time your joints creak, and your body aches, and you are all too aware of the weariness of our fragile existence, remember the glorious image of the prophet Ezekiel and start singing to yourself: "The knee bone's connected to the thigh bone. The thigh bone's connected to the hip bone. The hip bone's connected to the ... Now hear the word of the Lord!" For though we may be like dry bones before God, God is able to remake us in and by his life-giving power. That is good news for aging bodies.

But, more reflectively, and casting a deeper light back across the centuries of the Old Testament and forward into our own time, can we learn to read John 11 as a portrait of new life overcoming our tears about the old life? Yes, Jesus wept, and that is because there is real loss in all our struggles against the darkness of our world, even unto death. But at the same time, was Jesus so excited about this life-remaking power of God that he could barely wait to demonstrate it for Mary and Martha? And so it was that "the dead man came out" (v. 44). Then some believed, while others were reduced to "What are we to do?" (v. 47), because when this kind of power is at work, no one can sit idly by and just hope that it will all blow over. The story of Lazarus, in other words, is once again a story about all of us, and John's Gospel is once again a story about the reality of life (and death). Lazarus is a preview of the end. But the end is not yet.

CHAPTER 8

Jesus Gives Himself Away—John 13

Read John 13:1–17 and 31–35 (and
Exodus 12:1–4 and 12:11–14)

STORM CLOUDS ARE GATHERING in Jerusalem, and Jesus washes the disciples' feet.

Peter has a better idea: "Lord, not my feet only, but also my hands and my head" (v. 9).

Storm clouds are gathering in Egypt, and God introduces to Moses and Aaron the idea of Passover. Take only what you can carry. We leave at night. But, say the worried Israelites, only what we can carry? And where will we live? What do you mean, "In the wilderness?" We have a better idea: Can't we stay in Egypt?

Storm clouds are gathering—in Brussels, in London, in Washington DC, in our own backyards. The world we live in is heading for what feels like an out-of-control disaster, as hard to imagine as the end of the Roman Empire, the end of the British Empire, the end of the American Empire? And Jesus comes to wash the feet of his church. But wait. His church thinks it has a better idea.

Now tell me: what is wrong with that picture?

Let us keep it simple. The story of Jesus washing feet in John 13 has two main characters in it: Jesus and everybody else. Peter gets to play the lead role in the "everybody else" part. As do we. We are Peter. We are certainly not Jesus. So when Jesus washes Peter's feet, he washes our feet. But what does that mean?

Peter thinks (a) Jesus should not be doing this at all, since he is Jesus, after all; or (b) if he does have to, then surely he should wash every part of him. To the first point, Jesus says, "I know what I'm doing, Peter, but you don't," though he puts it a bit differently: "Unless I wash you, you have no share with me." To the second point, Jesus again says, "I know what I'm doing, Peter, but you don't," though this time his actual words are "One who has bathed does not need to wash, except for the feet, but is entirely clean." At the start of this little interchange, Jesus says to Peter, "You won't understand this yet, but you will later."

So what do we think? Presumably we might also say, "Jesus you should not be doing this. You are the great and mighty Lord of all the earth who should not be troubling yourself over a few people gathered here and there to remember you twenty centuries later." It can certainly be easy to lose sight of the bigger story—the bigger history—of which we are a part as Christian readers, if we are gathering with a handful of saints on a cold and wet winter's day, barely able to hear ourselves sing over the roar of the failing heating system. But I wonder if Jesus says, "Where else would I rather be?" Playing our part, we then respond: "In that case, Lord, we have quite a lot of issues and complaints and problems, and would like to take up your time with them, if that's okay with you?" But Jesus says, "Just the feet," adding that we are not going to understand, for now.

Peter models the constant temptation to go for all *or* nothing. We are either the strongest of people who do not need God's help *or* we are the worst of all, miserable offenders, and there is no health in us, as it was once put in the great Book of Common Prayer (a little unfortunately, in some people's opinion).

It is hard to get this right. Hard to hold the balance. We are quite like Peter. We think we know best. It turns out that there is a way to get the balance right, and Jesus is about to tell Peter what it is.

The key is in John's focus on how Jesus *serves* his disciples. Likewise, we should serve one another, and we should love one another. We should, to use the image of this passage, wash one another's feet. Our task is not to outthink Jesus and work out what he should or should not do. Our task is to pursue acts of faithful service and love. In the meantime, and through it all, guess who takes care of the bigger picture? This is a Gospel passage, so we hardly even need to use our chance to guess, because we know the answer: Jesus.

Every Easter, during Holy Week for those who celebrate that, usually on Maundy Thursday, many churches around the world remember this story as they enact their own services of foot-washing. I have been privileged to wash the feet of young and old in such services; feet across the whole range from elegant and well-kept to old and frail. To kneel before someone and wash their feet may be symbolic rather than a serious healthcare option, but it is a powerful and moving symbolic action. I have seen it bring tears to the eyes of those involved, myself included. Anyone who has taken the time to stop, participate, and celebrate, in such an action, is unlikely to ever say "It is merely symbolic." By no means: it is richly and emotionally symbolic. Maybe Jesus knew what he was doing when he used this action to symbolize service?

Maundy Thursday is a day celebrated in preparation for the barren trials of Good Friday. We stand poised right on the edge of the darkest of nights. This Passover meal that John has Jesus eating with his disciples feels like a last moment of familiarity before the story lurches into the vast emptiness of Jesus' death on the cross. All seems lost. But then again, on Easter morning, all will seem won again. Here the history of the church chimes with our own experience: we tend to emphasize one or the other. But it is almost as if Jesus, kneeling down to perform this simple, stunning act of washing our feet, says, "Let me take care of the bigger picture." Once again, I return to an earlier way of expressing the heart of the matter: the world is broken and we cannot fix it; and our own hearts will be broken, and we cannot fix them either; and this would be an impossible burden for us to bear, so Jesus chooses to bear it for us.

Then, after that, he does give us a part to play, a part that we *can* bear. Although I am sure that Jesus was able to predict that we would find it difficult. (You can almost hear Peter saying, "Never, Lord—I'll always play my part. I won't find it difficult," as Jesus says, "Remind me to tell you the one about the cock crowing when we have a minute.") The part that we have to play is simple: love one another. As we take up our task of living out the love that can change our world, each of us in our own ways, Jesus will take care of going to hell and back again, so that sin, death, and the devil do not have the last word.

Will we understand what Jesus is up to as we go about the business of playing our part? I think the answer is "no" much of the time. But can we have confidence that he is winning back the world for us, one act of love at a time? I think the answer is "yes," all the time, because the future of the world is in his hands, not ours. This is a relief, or as it has been more traditionally called in the church, "good news."

By the way, will we be constantly tempted to think that we have a better idea? Yes. But we do not.

Just once in a while, we get a glimpse of how our own acts of loving kindness contribute to the strange ways in which a man washing our feet is part of God healing the world. We cherish those glimpses, not least because they are not the material of everyday life, at least in the sense that they do not happen every day. In another sense, everyday life is precisely what they are, because they come in the midst of the daily round of eating, sleeping, working, and washing (one another's feet) that make up everyday existence. Here is one such glimpse I once had which, many years later, still never ceases to remind me of the joy of playing our part at the same time as the realization that we barely understand how our efforts fit into God's bigger work.

Once my wife and I had a friend in our church who was a single mother, living with her teenage son further down our street, a short cul-de-sac of small apartments. She has trouble getting by. She manages, because it is not that people do not care and look out for her, but we suspect that one thing she misses is the chance to have some extra money, and that once in a while that would be a nice gift for her. But perhaps money through her door would just get sucked into the weekly budget and, while that would no doubt help, it is not the joyous experience of being loved that we most want for her.

So we decide instead to buy a couple of boxes of food for her at the supermarket and leave them on her doorstep. We go for a mixture of basic things that will last, and some special treats that perhaps she would never buy, and load up two big banana boxes full of food. It is a lot of fun running around the food aisles trying to imagine what would be good gifts. I recommend it.

Our little street is full of people who seem to spend all evening looking out the window, so it is not till around midnight that most of the lights are out and I can go down the street unobserved. We had a small porch entrance to our house, and my plan is to leave the boxes in what I presume will be the identical porch to hers. Quietly I open the car, lift out two heavy-laden banana boxes, and carry them stealthily down the street. I am grinning all the way there: this is a truly joyful thing to do. Unfortunately, her house has no porch, since she has had an additional external door fitted, so after surveying all the options and mindful of being discovered, I simply leave the boxes outside the front door with her name written on them (just to be sure).

Walking back, I wonder if they will still be there in the morning, if her neighbor might find them first, or if it might unexpectedly pour with rain in the night, and a whole host of other things. But even these worries can't wipe away my grin. Back home, we lay in bed and pray a prayer of thankfulness for going through with the idea, and ask that what we had given will be helpful. We fall asleep with a rare peace at the thought of actually having done something right.

A week, maybe two weeks, later, this lady stands up in church. In God's good timing, we are not there, and we hear it secondhand. What we hear is that this lady told a story that eclipsed ours completely.

She was telling the story about a friend of hers who was in a poor way, struggling against an awkward family situation and a physical handicap, who was really having a hard time getting by. She told of how she had been trying to find a way to help her friend. What she had really wanted to do was set aside some food each week and give her friend a couple of boxes of food as a special way of sharing God's love with her. But she had not been able to, because her own situation was hard enough. Until one day, when she had walked out of the front door to go to work and found these two boxes sitting on her step, full of good gifts that she could pass on. At first she had thought it must be a mistake, but they even had her name written on them.

Her joy was real, and her story was richly emotional. We reflected: Was our own action a symbolic one—that is to say, in the midst of our continuing hardship, was there this small opportunity for joy? Yes, it was symbolic. But it was not merely symbolic. It was a transformative experience for us, for our friend, and then in turn for her friend, and indeed for the whole church, who listened in increasing amazement as she told the tale. It was as if someone had peeled back the grey skies, and allowed us all to see a little piece of the world to come.

See the life to which John 13 gives witness. As we serve one another, God remakes the world. As we love one another, God remakes the world. So hear these words of Jesus:

You call me Teacher and Lord—and you are right, for that is what I am. So if I, your Lord and Teacher, have washed your feet, you also ought to wash one another's feet. For I have set you an example, that you also should do as I have done to you. Very truly, I tell you, servants are not greater than their master, nor are messengers greater than the one who sent them. If you know these things, you are blessed if you do them.

This is the word of the Lord, so thanks be to God.

CHAPTER 9

Learning from Philip How Not to Understand—John 14

Read John 14:1–14

"Do not let your hearts be troubled." We are looking at a passage that, in a few short verses, will take in questions concerning Jesus being the only way, the relative identity of two persons of the trinity, the disciples doing greater works than Jesus, and getting whatever you pray for in Jesus' name. "Do not let your hearts be troubled," he says. What could possibly go wrong?

We meet Jesus here, in the first instance, through the lens of the apostle Philip. We do not know much about the apostle Philip—he was one of the twelve, and one of the more enigmatic people we come across in the Gospels. He is mentioned in four contexts in John, which is rather more than the other Gospels manage: all three of the others mention him once only in passing in a list of the disciples. But John elaborates. A brief review of the four contexts may be in order.

First, there is the incident at the fig tree that we mentioned back in chapter 1. Jesus finds Philip and says, "Follow me" (1:43). That's all. Not much narrative development there. Jesus is down by the Jordan, he has just gotten baptized, and he has decided that it is time to head up north, to Galilee. John writes: "He found Philip and said to him, 'Follow me.'" In turn, Philip finds Nathanael and says, "We found the one Moses wrote about—you know, in the prophets and the law. It's Jesus, from Nazareth"; this prompts Nathanael's famous response: "Can anything good come out of Nazareth?" Philip replied noncommittally, even tactfully: "Come and see." In turn, Nathanael is greeted generously by Jesus ("a true Israelite! in whom there is no guile!"—with Jesus momentarily switching to the King James Version), but this makes him a bit suspicious: "How do you know about me?" Jesus says, "I saw you under the fig tree, before Philip called you." Something about the way this conversation goes suggests to me that whatever Nathanael was up to under the fig tree was not very edifying—but anyway, Philip drops out of the story at this point. Jesus, meanwhile, may have been left pondering that if Nathanael was so impressed by being seen under a fig tree, then it was going to prove complicated to get on to some of the bigger issues that he was hoping to introduce them to in due course.

Second, in John 6, there is the ad hoc festival up a mountain. Five thousand people come to a small seminar booked into a tent that will only hold twelve, and the only catering provided is five loaves and two small fish. (Though John does not record this, there are also no functioning bathroom facilities—some things never change.) Anyway, watching them come up and sit around him, a large crowd gathering, Jesus turns to our man Philip and says, "Where are we going to get bread for all this lot?" John tells us that this was to test Philip, who—noncommittally; tactfully; and possibly panicking inside, thinking, "Well if *he* doesn't know . . ."—says,

"Six months wages would not sort this out." At which point Andrew takes over, and the rest is history—or at least, the rest is deeply significant symbolic narrative. Nothing further is said about Philip's role in it all, though.

His third starring moment is in chapter 12: Jesus enters into Jerusalem, amidst rumors, excitement, confusion, and everything rushing to a head. Some Greeks come to Philip (12:21) and say, "Sir, we wish to see Jesus." At this point, Philip, a man of action, a decisive word upon his lips as always, goes and tells Andrew, who says (something like) "Let's go and tell Jesus," who, in turn, says, "The hour has come!" This turns out to be quite a key moment, for Jesus, for John's Gospel, indeed for the whole history of the human race; but as for Philip's part, he kept his head down. Again.

Which brings us to the passage at hand: John 14. "Do not let your hearts be troubled." Jesus' mighty farewell discourse. Several chapters of the most extraordinary teaching in all of Holy Scripture. We are deep into the mysteries of John's Gospel now, and have left Matthew, Mark, and Luke behind, heading out into the Johannine kingdom, where Jesus and the Father are one, the kind of oneness that is "of one being and substance with the father"—begotten, not made. More specifically, Jesus is going to prepare a place for us. "Do not let your hearts be troubled. In my Father's house are many mansions." That does sound like a big house. Some modern translations find this so improbable that they whittle it down to "in my Father's house there are many rooms," which makes heaven sound a bit like an extended guest house, whereas, most likely, Jesus was talking big, rather bigger than we can easily imagine: my Father has a place so spacious that it incorporates within it many dwelling places, which are in turn as spacious as mansions themselves. His model here is the old extended homestead of ancient Israel, where new branches of the family unit build on their own dwelling to the family home, their own place within the father's house: no building permits or planning permission needed. Jesus prepares a place for us, and what a wonderful place it is going to be. Everyone gets their own mansion, at the same time as everyone gets to be together. This is good news. Magnificent news, in fact. Let not your hearts be troubled. He has got your accommodation sorted.

He is also on top of transport: "I will go and prepare a place for you, and I will come again and take you there with me." So now you also know how you are going to get there.

"Not so fast!" says Thomas. "We do not know where you are going, and how can we know how to follow you?" Jesus patiently explains: "Yes, Thomas, you do know the way—were you not listening? I am taking you, stick with me, I am the way: stick with me and you will get to where you need to go." We in the twenty-first century feel the pull at this point of a whole other conversation, on "Are there other ways to get to where we want to go?" Of course, Jesus does not stop to address this, although my best guess is that he would want to say that the destination is not a place, such that we might all download the map-reference and make our own arrangements to meet him there, but the destination is a relationship with the Father—i.e., the Father of our Lord Jesus Christ, and that requires a life that is lived along the way of the cross. In fact, it requires precisely the life that Jesus is in the process of modeling for them in John's Gospel as he teaches them on this darkest of nights. That is the only life that will get you there: hence, Jesus says, "I am the life."

LEARNING FROM PHILIP HOW NOT TO UNDERSTAND—JOHN 14

What is more, his words at this point are entirely trustworthy, hence his "I am the truth"; and when we want to press even further and say "Yes, but what about those others," his only word is "Do not let your hearts be troubled." He has transport and accommodation sorted: can we let him take care of other people's bookings too?

We arrive back at Philip. "Lord," says Philip, in verse 8, his final starring role in John's Gospel, "Lord, show us the Father, and we will be satisfied." Good old Philip. Still noncommittal. Still tactful. Eager to please. A nice line in asking questions. But what is it he wants to know? What more is there to know than all that Jesus has just been telling them? He is the way, he is the truth, he is the life—is there some further revelation that Philip thinks he needs? Some further training? Some further instruction?

Jesus says to him, gently but firmly, "Philip, remember who you are talking to. Whoever has seen me has seen the Father." There is no more. No further revelation. We have what we need in Jesus.

Philip's mind flashes back to the incident at the fig-tree, and he realizes: Jesus *saw*. He saw Nathanael, and he already knew; and he saw the life he was calling them to, and they followed. In the feeding of the five thousand, Jesus *saw* those crowds, and knew there was no food, but he wanted Philip to see, and he drew him into the work he was already doing. He had it in hand, and now Philip sees. As for the Greeks who wanted to see Jesus, Philip had gotten them there (though not very confidently), but Jesus had already seemed to know about it, and now Philip sees. And here, in John 14, as Jesus patiently answers Philip—determined, eager to please, always ready with the helpful follow-up question—finally

Philip *sees*. He sees that to see Jesus is enough, that there is no additional mystery to be revealed.

At least, that is my guess. If it is true that there is no further mention of the apostle Philip, then all we have to go on is that he did not ask any more questions, and come Acts 1, he is still one of the twelve disciples, getting ready to launch out into the church at the beginning of the new creation. There is the possibility that the Philip who converted the Ethiopian in Acts 8 is the same Philip—it seems unlikely to me, but not impossible—and if so, well, look at him run. He has come a long way.

Jesus did say, back in John 14, that the one who believes in him would do greater works than Jesus himself, though by this point in the passage the "you" that Jesus is talking to is plural and not just Philip himself. If this is one of Jesus' truthful sayings, as he seems to be emphasizing here in chapter 14, then that is quite a statement: greater works than Jesus himself! This does not mean, I am sure, more spectacular, or somehow more miraculous works—as if Jesus may have put a coin in the fish's mouth, but we will build an entire banking system out of thin air. But I take it that it means that where Jesus has been testifying on his own behalf (John 8:18), those of us who follow him in his way will be able to testify even to his resurrection from the dead. Or, in other words, Jesus is pointing forward to an unglimpsed reality that we, in the church, can now point to in all its fullness: new life, new creation, new heavens, and new earth. Let not your hearts be troubled!

My final guess is that when Jesus closes this passage with "If in my name you ask me for anything, I will do it," he is carrying on the same line of thought: if those who come after him continue his work, then prayer is about the ongoing

LEARNING FROM PHILIP HOW NOT TO UNDERSTAND—JOHN 14

commitment to identify ourselves with the work that Jesus himself continues to do through us. In the words of the well-known theologian Mick Jagger, "You can't always get what you want, but if you try sometimes, you might find that you get what you need."

That is enough guessing for one passage. Of course, the reason why we have had to guess is that there is so much that John does not tell us. But I have wanted to take seriously, and at face value, Jesus' opening words: "Do not let your hearts be troubled." So there is good news; the same good news that the prophet Isaiah foretold, that speaks of a God who knows the end from the beginning and who meets us, wherever we are, with comfort and assurance. Jesus would have had plenty of reasons to worry as he tried to pass on his visionary teaching, on the night before he was betrayed. But instead he chooses to bless us with the remarkable, gospel-shaped gift of a confidence we did not deserve, and courage to press on in the face of much that we do not understand.

One Easter, on a Good Friday that we were marking with the local churches together in our hometown, I was part of a group making our small quiet walk of witness into the market square, where we would sing a hymn and recall some of the gospel story. It was an annual moment of offering a public testimony, fairly unobtrusively, that the real world is God's world, and that the most important story is God's story. It is unspectacular, but it is faithful. On one such particularly memorable occasion, I noticed two things. One was that a large man with a clipboard was going around trying to sign people up for financial products, and he was accompanied by a tall guy in a teddy bear suit. I thought it is surely not fair that people look at a place like this square and think that Christians marking Easter are the ones who are weird while the teddy bear in a suit selling home insurance is perfectly normal. But there was a second thing, which has to do with a man who regularly proclaims the King James Version out loud in our town, which I do not think is necessarily the way to go on the whole. He just happened to be reading from John's passion narrative on the steps of the statue in the market square at the precise moment that our procession of a hundred or so people gathered around the statue for our planned public act of worship. As he read, it dawned on him that—for probably the first time in his life—he had gathered a large, attentive and entirely sympathetic crowd. Of course, we all thought at first that he was with us and was the first reader in our worship service. But as he looked up, completely taken aback, he said, "I see I have gathered quite a crowd." He smiled, announced his own opinion (doubtless not shared by anyone else in the square) that he had been reading from the one true Bible version, the King James, and he went on his way. I thought: that is the way the kingdom of God works, gathering up his one small—perhaps even debatable—act of witness into a sudden massive gathering of the faithful standing with him in public. You think you know how you are going to play your part, but God plays it through you in ways you could not ask or imagine.

To Philip, and possibly to all the disciples, perhaps it looked as if everything was being lost. But we are privileged to see part of the bigger picture. Amidst all the many things we hear in this life, let us hear the words of our Lord Jesus Christ, these extraordinary words of assurance: "Do not let your hearts be troubled. Believe in God; believe also in me." What a gift Jesus left us on the night before he was betrayed.

CHAPTER 10

Beyond the Dying of the Light: Resurrection—John 20

Read John 20:1–18

JOHN 20 IS WRITTEN in a curious, pressing mixture of present tense exploration and past tense "telling you what happened," almost as if the storyteller is so overwhelmed by what he is saying that he can barely pause to get his points in order, although actually—almost certainly—it is a deliberate effect. John is the master storyteller, telling you the most masterful story of all time, and he wants you to feel the sheer wonder of it. Relive the sense of discovery: run to the tomb with him, with Peter, with Mary. "Come with me!" he pleads. "Come with me and I will show you the moment when it all exploded into life."

So we go. I will try and capture the sense of hanging on for the firm ground of clarity, as the story swirls and swells its way around that first Easter morning.

We are on our way. It is the first day of the week. Mary Magdalene comes early. The disorientation of the soon-to-pass darkness, the dawn at the beginning of a new world. Early she comes. She sees the stone: it is taken from the tomb. So she runs. In the darkness she sees the stone not where it is

81

supposed to be, and she is not going in to look, but running now the other way, and she comes to Simon Peter, and—here I cut a long story short and simplify—to a disciple that I am going to call John, though here (and indeed often through the Gospel) he describes himself as the one whom Jesus loved. So she comes to Peter and to John, and she says, breathless I imagine, for the new breath of life had not yet been breathed upon them, she says "They've taken . . . the Lord . . . from the tomb . . . and we don't know . . . where they've put him." She has her hands down on her knees, struggling to talk, like an Olympic athlete being interviewed after breaking the 200-meter sprint record, not exactly eloquent, but urgent.

Peter and John shoot off, like a cork out of a resurrection bottle, and they are running together. Peter's ahead, now John, now Peter—it is like the Oxford-Cambridge boat race out there, but John is faster! It is John in first! Tell us John, talk us through that last hundred meters . . . But John is not talking. He stoops down, peering in as the light is starting to improve. He sees linen cloths lying there, but he does not go in. Just at that moment, Simon Peter comes charging up, a bit more out of shape than John, but also, famously, problematically (but marvelously), bolder than John, and in he charges. John has a bit of storytelling fun here, having earlier patiently explained that, from outside the tomb, he "sees lying there linen cloths," he now writes that as Peter charged all the way in, he also "sees lying there linen cloths." But in another way, Peter does get a better view, because he sees also another cloth, from Jesus' head, not lying with the linen cloths. Now John comes in, this time describing himself (with a small modest cough) as "the one having come first to the tomb," and now finally, after all this running and seeing and not seeing and wondering and waiting and the swell of divine mystery and the sheer building excitement of it all, we read, at last, in short and simple words right there in the last part of verse 8: "and he saw . . . and he believed."

It has taken eight verses to build up to the straightforward subject and verb that we have been waiting for. I do not think John wrote this breathlessly, but I do think he wrote it to catch us up in the breathlessness of it. He saw, and he believed. What did he see? Hard to say, actually. Perhaps the clue was in the folded graveclothes. In other words, the absence of a body did not equate to the body having been stolen, but to something else; something not stated here, but which adds up for John to some sort of vindication. He did not just see graveclothes, let us say, but he *saw the point*. The John who was there at the tomb, sitting at his desk in his old age, writing it out one more time, sits back and stares at the new dawn, at the far horizon, and the biggest smile in human history breaks out once more on his face. He wants to say "You had to be there!" but the next best thing is that he can tell you just what it was like.

On reflection, he adds in the next verse, since he has been reflecting on this moment for pretty much his whole life ever since, on reflection we had not understood up until that point, for we had not seen that Scripture itself (or the Old Testament, in our terms) had been saying that the messiah had to rise from the dead. On reflection, yes, we see now how the Old Testament had been saying this all along. But on that darkened morning, sweaty, exhausted, and confused at the tomb, hardly daring to believe the evidence of their eyes, it took running in and realizing that the tomb was empty, and that Jesus was on his way somewhere else. To the Father, in fact, as we will see in a few verses. "And he saw ... and he believed." O happy day.

Now recall, there had been someone else running, looking, and not understanding: Mary Magdalene. Earlier in John's gospel Mary had been the one who first got to the tomb, then ran off and raised the alarm, and then had presumably followed Peter and John back, though possibly not quite at their speed, since she had already run that race once that morning. We pick up her story again in verse 11. She is outside weeping. Then she also stoops to look into the tomb. That word "stooped," or "bent low," is used by John in verse 5 to describe himself peering into the tomb, and now he uses it again to describe Mary peering into the tomb. Is it just an incidental detail that suggests that if you want to see Jesus, if you want to be taken to the place where it begins to make sense, that you might have to stoop down low, to bow down, to be willing to lower yourself to a position where you might really see what is going on? Even if John did not quite mean all that, it is a thought that fits with where this story is going.

Mary sees two angels. On another day, that would be the headline. Maybe these angels had taken this particular job thinking it would be their starring moment, and in a way it is, but they are about to be upstaged; in fact, they have been upstaged already by the observation that they are sitting at the head and the feet of a man who is no longer there: the Jesus who is not any longer lying in the tomb. I cannot help pondering the celestial conversation as this job was handed out: "I want you to guard Jesus, only he will not be there." They say, "Are you sure, Lord? Won't that look a bit strange?" God says, "Believe me, you looking strange is not going to be top of anyone's agenda today. Just get on with it."

So these angels say to her, in a phrase that sounds a bit odd to us, "Woman, why do you weep?" (I note that this is even how the Message translation puts it.) Where I live, in the North of England, this would equate to "Y'alright, pet?" (though strangely none of the commentaries I consulted thought of this equivalent phrase).

But Mary is not all right. "They have taken away my Lord, and I do not know where they have laid him." John slips back into his pressing, breathless present tense at this point, when he writes (after she turned around) "and she sees Jesus, standing there." Only she does not know that it is Jesus. Well, she wouldn't, would she? Her brain is turning somersaults at this point. First, what is with the tomb being open? Secondly, what are Peter and John up to? Now, admittedly, it is hard to match up the story of "Peter and John in the tomb" with this one, but here is how I read it (though there are other ways too). Mary is peering in from the outside while the men are doing the important detective work with the cloths, only Mary is seeing angels and chatting to external witnesses. There is a whole different angle there on who sees what and how significant it is that it is the woman who really sees, from a distance, while the men wade in. I picture the angels looking rather distastefully at these big men clumping around in their sacred space, and deciding to talk to Mary instead. Again, I could not find a commentary that backed me up on this.

Meanwhile, thirdly, Mary is now seeing someone in the garden, and no matter who it is, she is simply not going to recognize him at this precise moment. Until, that is, he draws her in to a conversation. He too begins with, "Y'alright, pet?"

85

Then: "What's up, love?"—more usually translated as "Whom do you seek?" That voice is starting to sound familiar.

She pleads: "Sir." Interestingly, the word is *kyrie*, the same word that means "Lord" and that she herself used when she had said to Peter and John that her Lord had been taken from the tomb. "Sir, if you have carried him away, tell me where you have placed him, and I will take him."

Verse 16: Jesus says to her, "Mary."

She says, "Rabbi."

It is enough. John has to tell *us* what it means, that she is speaking in Hebrew, that it means "teacher," but it is enough to communicate what Mary needs to say at this point, which, roughly paraphrased, is "It *is* you." Personally, I am guessing she throws her arms around him at this point and gives him the first hug of the new creation, she not being the quiet and reserved type, and noting also that Jesus next says something like "Stop clinging to me." (In Matthew 28, Mary Magdalene takes hold of the risen Jesus' feet at this point, so perhaps "hug" is a bit of a loose interpretation; but it *is* a spontaneous moment of overwhelmed worship and thankfulness as much as anything else.) It turns out that there are complicated theological reasons why she is not supposed to be hugging him at this point. Even so, according to Holy Scripture, when it comes to loving Jesus, it seems like the hug comes first, and the theology comes second; or—if you are not persuaded about the hug—the worship and thankfulness come first, and the theology second. Indeed, might we even do well to think of "theology" as basically being worship seeking understanding?

Is it possible to see the truth about Jesus unless you are right there with Mary Magdalene—the Mary that Luke once described as "the Mary from whom seven demons had come out" (Luke 8:2), the Mary with a past, the Mary whose own experience can match our own pain and shame, whatever it is we may or may not have done? Is it possible to see the truth about Jesus unless we too are willing to give him the twenty-first-century resurrected equivalent of a hug? What Jesus says next is glorious: "My Father and your Father; my God and your God," reminding me, rather interestingly, of the words of another woman of faith who truly saw what it was all about: Ruth, telling Naomi that she will love and follow her forever ("Your God will be my God," Ruth 1:16). Jesus' words here will keep the theologians in business for twenty centuries and still counting, and John, for one, is even trying to work out the implications as he is writing his Gospel, but Mary herself goes away and announces to the disciples—or rather, as John puts it so beautifully, "Here comes Mary Magdalene . . . announcing to the disciples," and he has her using short and simple words once again to get at the heart of the wondrous tale. She says, "I have seen the Lord."

Sing choirs of angels! Sing in exultation! Jesus, the Lord, is risen from the dead. All stories end and then start again here. Our lives are caught up in the response to the risen Christ that has been going on these past two thousand years. We never leave behind the race to the tomb, the mysterious absence, the moment of truth, the *seeing and believing*. If our Christian faith is not somehow informed and sustained, energized and powered by the resurrection of Christ, then—to use a phrase John himself might have used—we do not know what we are missing.

Christ is risen! Hallelujah!

The resurrection is what it is all about. The New Testament goes further: it is not that this is the twist in the tale after things were seeming to get away from God for a bit as he struggled to work out how to deal with the Babylonians or the Romans. Rather, what they come to realize as the New Testament unfolds is that the resurrection is what it was always about: the sheer impossibility of the God of life being limited by the constraints of death in some final, defeating way. Of course, death is real, horrible, and disastrous. There is always Good Friday to remind us that God is with us in our darkest days. But the God of Abraham, Isaac, and Jacob, the God of our Lord Jesus Christ, is the God of life, who—on that first Easter morning—finally revealed in plain sight that in a head-to-head between death and Jesus, Jesus wins. Resurrection is the power of life, and it has always gone deeper, reached further, and lasted longer than the power of death. And this is what it was *always* all about.

Remember with me: the God who made human life out of the breath-less dust of the earth; the God who delivered his people Israel out of the deathly grind of slavery; the God who gave sacrifices to take away the sins of his people and destroy those sins out in the wilderness; the God who gave a land to be a place of peace as a respite from danger—Jerushalom, the city of peace; the God who delivered the struggler out of the depths in Psalm 22, lifting him up to praise the God who will be honored long after the rich of this earth have gone down to the dust, as resurrection hope bursts out of the heart of an ancient Israelite psalm; the God who sent his mighty wind or breath or spirit (his *ruach*) on the dead army in the valley of dry bones in the book of Ezekiel, and raised them back to life. Remember all this great crowd of

(Old Testament) witnesses, because God is and was and always shall be the God of resurrection life.

This is why we have hope. This is why there is a church. This is why we celebrate. This is why, when we open our mouths to sing, our voices are caught up into a song of praise so much bigger than we can imagine; whether it is number forty-one in the green hymnal sung by two or three tone-deaf elderly saints to the accompaniment of the church hall organ; or the newest songs from the best worship band in the country; or even Aslan singing the new world of Narnia into creation. I once participated in a Sing-Along *Messiah* at the Royal Albert Hall in London, a fact as true as it is unlikely to my friends who have heard me sing: a performance of Handel's *Messiah* designed for audience participation, i.e. sung by anyone who wanted to turn up and join in on the day.

I remember listening to a battered old cassette, back in those days, staring blankly at the sheet music in preparation, and wondering just how long it would take to get to the hallelujah chorus (most of the evening). I caught the tube train up to central London, feeling tired and a bit out of my comfort zone, and I vividly recall standing to sing at the appropriate moment, my poorly rehearsed bass line more or less ready, and the whole Royal Albert Hall erupted into this most spectacular flood of praise, and my spirit was lifted so far and so fast that I all but cried with joy right there and then. That is what the resurrection does for our lives, our voices, and our hearts. It catches us up into God's amazing work of new creation, recreation, reorientation, and new life. You open your mouth, thinking you know how you are going to perform your part, but God performs it through you in ways you could not ask or imagine.

Because all of this is true, we have hope. Because John, Peter, and Mary came to the tomb two thousand years ago and realized that the story they had thought was ending was actually beginning in a whole new way—because of what they passed on to us from that first Easter morning—we have hope. Because this is good news (the gospel) for all people everywhere, we have hope.

I wonder if we can too easily live with a kind of fear that our own stories are ending; a desire to hold on to what God has been doing in our lives so far because we cannot quite see the future. Do we often have an overpowering worry that God, who has been doing fairly well over many centuries, may have finally met his match in our own particular combination of cares and concerns and complex circumstances? To such fears and insecurities, the resurrection says this: when we have plenty to worry about, then it turns out there is an even bigger reason to have hope; when it looks like our stories are ending, they may be beginning in whole new ways. That is the thing with the God of resurrection life: you never know what he might do next.

CONCLUDING REFLECTION

An Essay on Spiritual Reading and John

THERE ARE MANY WAYS to read the Bible. Not all of them are helpful.

What I have tried to model in this book is helpful reading, which I have called spiritual reading. It is reading that is determined to locate the word of life, determined to hold on for a blessing, convinced that God has more for us than encouragement and exhortation (though not less than that). At the end of the introduction, I said that "There is no better way to pursue the practice of spiritual reading than to engage in it." But now that we have engaged in it, what lessons might we take away regarding how to go about it in future? Is there any guidance?

Therefore, this conclusion takes a little step back from the presentation and purpose of the other chapters, and asks what spiritual reading—and, in particular, what spiritual reading of John—is about.

Thoughtful Reading

The first thing to say is that spiritual reading, like all good reading, needs to be thoughtful and attentive reading, taking heed of the specific details in the text. To read John, for example, is to let the words of John's Gospel set the agenda for our reading, and not to use John as a convenient echo chamber for what we want to focus on. When we say "let John's Gospel set the agenda," this involves letting John speak first in the conversation we have with the Gospel of John. Of course, it is true that every reader brings their own perspectives and ideas to the reading, their own questions and concerns, and these will allow different readers to see different things. Clearly there is more than one way to read John. But if the reading is indeed a reading *of John*, then John has to have a leading voice in the conversation.

I hope this image of a conversation with the biblical text may allow us to avoid two extremes. One extreme is to say that, in the end, all our interests are irrelevant, and our job is solely to get the right answer about what John means (or meant). The other extreme is to say that whatever I am interested in as a reader is all that counts, and whether John intended it or not is irrelevant. Instead, I suggest thinking of entering into a conversation with John where we pay him the courtesy of listening first, and then responding and bringing our own questions into dialogue with him and his text. For myself, the role of the Gospel of John as part of Holy Scripture suggests that a good deal of deference as a reader is appropriate. In other words, it will be a conscious part of our reading of John that we want it to challenge, and guide and inform us. We therefore need all the help we can get in slowing down and paying attention to the particular ways that John uses words and phrases, ideas and echoes—patiently drawing us into a new understanding that will most likely be different from the one we had when we started reading. Probably, if you have read this far, you are happy with that kind of suggestion. But we could also acknowledge that there are a range of possibilities for any such conversation; even discussions between the best of friends and the most generous-spirited of conversation partners can sometimes involve disagreement and a struggle to see things the same way.

The particular point I would like to emphasize about spiritual reading being "thoughtful reading" is that it does involve making use of the best information we can find on matters of detail: questions about what specific words mean; about historical setting of the stories; about what we can know (if anything) about how and why the book was written, and how the author intended to handle matters of history and theology. These concerns make up the bundle of questions asked by biblical scholars under the heading of "historical criticism," or indeed other kinds of biblical criticism. Such approaches have been followed both helpfully and unhelpfully over the years. Although it would take a much longer discussion to sort this out properly, I find the following rule of thumb helpful. Historical criticism is of great value in sharpening our appreciation of what is going on in the text, and guarding against simply assuming that what the text is talking about is what we already thought it must be talking about. Historical and critically minded approaches do well at emphasizing unfamiliar angles, or pointing out historical or cultural data that we probably would not have known otherwise. All of this helps us avoid just trying to fit the text in to what we believed in the first place, because it makes it seem a bit strange or foreign to us. However, on the other hand, historical-critical approaches are a disappointing master. They are a problem when they reduce the enjoyment of many texts to matters of background detail and did-you-know-type passing observations, not all of which turn out to be as well-founded as you might think as scholarship goes on its way digging deeper, wider, and more sharply.

Therefore, I have tended to make use of historical-critical approaches to John's Gospel in all sorts of ways in the readings offered. But I have not found them sufficient to arrive at the kinds of reading I was seeking, readings that allow the text to probe and provoke us on a spiritual and practical level in terms of what it means to live in the light of John's Gospel today. The temptation for people who agree with such a claim (who think therefore that historical criticism tends to be quite limited) has been to under-estimate the usefulness of historical-critical approaches as aids to thoughtful reading. My contrary claim is therefore simply stated like this: spiritual reading is not the avoidance of historical, cultural, critical, and other approaches, but the making use of them under a bigger overarching banner that takes broader spiritual and theological concerns into account. Indeed, the related interest of recent years in the "theological interpretation of Scripture" is exactly the kind of approach I have found most useful. Readers who would like to see where that leads more generally are probably best helped by the excellent set of essays found in Davis's and Hays's *The Art of Reading Scripture*.[1]

---

1. Ellen F. Davis and Richard B. Hays, eds., *The Art of Reading Scripture* (Grand Rapids: Eerdmans, 2003).

AN ESSAY ON SPIRITUAL READING AND JOHN

The Real Jesus

The second thing to say is specific to interpreting a Gospel, and perhaps especially specific to interpreting John's Gospel. It is that the Jesus we are seeking to meet in and through John is *the real Jesus*. We know this real Jesus, if we know Jesus at all, through a range of ways, including in prayer, in worship, and in taking bread and wine, all of which are mediated to us via our participation in the life of the church. We also know this Jesus through reading Scripture, which is less directly mediated to us through the church, and through our historical analysis of what we know about Jesus, the man from Galilee. This last approach is sometimes called "the quest of the historical Jesus" (mainly because of a major early twentieth-century book of that name). Readers may well have encountered it, either in helpful books that explore what we know or in sermons that cannot resist the line about "actually, if you know the background to this story, it turns out to mean something very relevant in its first-century context." I enjoy such books and sermons, since I am a Bible scholar and I do not get out much. But you will have realized, including via the discussion of "thoughtful reading" in this book, that I do not think that they offer a *better* way in to reading John's Gospel than the other approaches.

I am indebted here to the masterly discussion of Luke Timothy Johnson in his fine and still too-little-read book *The Real Jesus*.[2] Johnson distinguishes between the Jesus we know by historical reconstruction and the whole person of Jesus, known to Christians as the second person of the Holy

---

2. Luke Timothy Johnson, *The Real Jesus: The Misguided Quest for the Historical Jesus and the Truth of the Traditional Gospels* (San Francisco: Harper San Francisco, 1996).

Trinity. We should be able to relate these two together. Most people who have explored this, in practice, tend to place all the emphasis on one or the other. I have tried to keep a balance. We must be willing to learn from the biblical text, or else there is probably not much point in reading it. But we need not pretend that we come to the biblical text without our own prior working assumptions and understandings, and as long as these are open to correction, we should probably do well not to set them completely to one side in our reading. So in practice, Christian convictions about Jesus that we learn in and through our life in the church have a helpful (though not infallible) role to play in shaping the way we read Gospel narratives. At the same time, the details of the text have a role to play in refining and reshaping our Christian convictions. Which comes first: the Bible or the teaching of the church? Both. Or neither, in the sense that each is formative for the other one. The Bible, or at least the New Testament, represents selected early-church understanding written down. The church's understanding is the reception of the Bible in God's ever-changing history. It is an exciting challenge to read the Bible in dialogue with our Christian convictions, and not let either one ride like a steamroller over the other as if it had nothing to contribute. Readers might want to reflect on whether the spiritual readings offered in this book successfully managed to navigate that path.

The Real Truth

This leads me on to a broader reflection on how biblical narratives work, as they bring us face-to-face with the real world. By "the real world," I mean the world understood as God would have us engage with it. Clearly there are plenty of other alternative ways to conceive of the world in which we live, but for Christian readers seeking spiritual wisdom, I cannot see that they should hold a greater claim on us.

In several of the readings offered here, I have tried to make a careful claim that—on the one hand—the story narrated by John may very well have happened roughly along the lines he draws for us; while, on the other hand, this is not the most significant thing about it. Jesus turned water into wine, or walked on the water, or in the end vacated the grave to leave an empty tomb. In all these cases, I have not had any particular issue with thinking that this happened, and that the Gospel narrative gets us somewhere near the ballpark of reading an account of what happened. But equally, and to my mind more significantly, I do not think it matters in most of these cases how close to the ballpark it gets us, or how exactly the text relates to the history behind it. Because that is not the issue with understanding what the text is trying to tell us.

One of the interesting things that has happened over the history of the church's interpretation of narratives like the ones we have looked at in John is that the focus has gradually slipped away from attending to what picture is drawn out for us by the text to trying to assess how far that picture matches up with what happened. This is true whether interpreters have wanted to defend the historical accuracy of the text or critique it. In either case, more or less equally, the focus is on the link between the text and history. In writing about this long story of the development of biblical interpretation, Hans Frei argued that this shift towards concerns with whether the narrative was historically descriptive actually represented a shift away from traditional concerns with what the narrative was saying. The book in which he argued this is a lengthy historical analysis of the phenomenon, and not for the faint-hearted.[3] But its central argument is easy to grasp. Our typically modern concern with historical accuracy, for all its interest and potential gains in our overall picture of what happened and how it matters, does not help us to read biblical narratives all that well. It "eclipses" their point and purpose in the shadow of other kinds of concerns about truth. If we are not alert to this, we end up saying that the truth is "what happened," in which case the purpose of the biblical text is to get us to somewhere else. In that view, the biblical text is more like a means of transport to the ancient world, allowing us to imagine that we sit in the presence of the action, unmediated to us by a narrator (itself the work of an author) offering an interpretation of what is going on. Notice that, on this understanding, the text itself has stopped being the prime focus of attention—it has become almost a dispensable step along the way to getting us to focus somewhere else. We are being encouraged to look past or away from the text. But, in contrast, I am pursuing Frei's interest in getting us to look not past or away from the text, but at it. How the author chooses the words to paint the picture, and how the scriptural canon locates each "painting" within the art gallery that is the collected Bible, makes a difference. If our goal is to learn what the *text* is telling us, then it is the text that is our focus. I entertain the modest hope that this simple observation might not sound self-defeatingly obvious.

Its implications, however, offer some helpful ways forward when it comes to reading a biblical narrative for a word

---

3. Hans W. Frei, *The Eclipse of Biblical Narrative: A Study in Eighteenth and Nineteenth Century Hermeneutics* (New Haven: Yale University Press, 1974).

of life. To draw together some of the various points being made in this concluding reflection: The key issue concerning how historical background information helps us is in informing and refining our imaginative engagement with the story. I think a useful illustration of this point is the phenomenon of the commentary track on a film that you buy, or a "making of" feature. Those who have enjoyed the film or the TV show that is thus blessed with these additional features may spend many happy hours watching extra details, learning how the effects were achieved, and hearing what it was like to put the final product together. The question, then, is: does this extra information help you enjoy the film any better? The answer is probably "yes" in some ways and "no" in others. Learning how the director or writer tried to represent a historical incident, if that is a relevant category for the film in question, can be illuminating. It can also be a tangent. You end up knowing about something other than the story that the film tells. Instead, you end up being an expert on "how they did it." That is why I am nervous of the frequent preacher's or teacher's trick of trying to explain a biblical narrative by introducing into the interpretation some data that comes from outside the text itself. When I say I am nervous of it, I do not mean that it should not be done. Just that it needs to be done carefully. Perhaps an example will clarify.

Suppose your goal is to read and contemplate the narrative about Jesus at the well in John 4. Scholars sometimes point out the socially shocking detail that Jesus is talking alone with the Samaritan woman, engaged in quite a deep discussion with her about life and how to live it. This is socially shocking, they may say, because we need to understand that a man did not usually talk alone with a woman in that culture. It seems to transgress social boundaries. In the light of the "woman at the well" theme from the Old Testament, which we mentioned in our reading of the story, maybe this opens up an angle concerning Jesus' intention to break social boundaries, or to make a radical statement about the value of women as full conversation partners despite cultural expectations that they were not, and so forth. All of these seem to me to be reasonable conjectures about the first century world and how an action such as that of Jesus in this story might have been understood. I think there is even good news for women in the particular detail that Jesus graces one such woman with a lengthy personal conversation about these weighty matters, and as such, I mentioned in passing this aspect of the story in the reading offered.

Now a reader unaware that this was an issue in the first century would miss this. But it seems to me that in so doing they would not necessarily miss the point of the story itself, with its concern for Jesus being the focus of our love, or our devotion, and indeed the source of our "living water," which were some of the issues I did try to draw out in the reading.

On the other hand, a reader unaware that the Old Testament offered several examples of a man encountering a woman at the well, which is where our reading began, would (I think) miss something of real importance in the point of the text. For it is partly the recognition of serious encounters at life-changing moments taking place at meeting points like the well, and how they have been depicted through the Old Testament, that equips readers to come to John 4 with the right sorts of questions about what they are expected to notice.

In short, the most important background for spiritual reading of the Bible is . . . the rest of the Bible. With the New

AN ESSAY ON SPIRITUAL READING AND JOHN

Testament, I am convinced that the best preparation is to read the Old Testament. Other backgrounds are available—and some of them are, in an ad hoc sort of way, very helpful. But what is conveyed to us in and through Scripture adds up to the whole art gallery within which our particular painting offers its particular perspective. Of course, the pressures of life do not allow us to stay in the art gallery forever, and we have to return to the routines of daily living. But if the visit to the art gallery (or the museum, or the cinema, or the theme park) is worth anything, it is because it illuminates our lives and helps us to see our daily routines differently, with the aid of those other stories (paintings, exhibits, etc.).

Readers may now realize why, back at the beginning of the book, I said that the "background information" you need for reading John is about its role in the biblical canon first, and only then (and only insofar as we ever know it) its historical origin second.

To summarize: we are invited to take seriously the extraordinary Christian claim that the real world is the world portrayed for us in Scripture. Truth is defined in those terms. History is an interesting subset of that truth, sometimes well-equipped to aid our comprehension, though often—at least in my view—not as well equipped as one might think. The Jesus that Christians are invited to follow is the real Jesus. John's Gospel, of all books ever written, is probably most obviously in support of such a view. If we ever get tired of such a fascinating quest, there are other interesting historical quests that are also on offer.

The special case of the resurrection might require a range of specific ways of putting these points carefully, since as the apostle Paul reminds us: "if Christ has not been raised then

... your faith has been in vain" (1 Cor 15:14). So Christians may with confidence insist that it matters historically that Christ was raised. Even so, note that the Gospel resurrection narratives are actually quite reluctant to speculate on what happened in the tomb. As careful readers have long noted, we never really find out how the resurrection happened, only that death is not the end and that Jesus is still alive. So it still seems unhelpful to suggest that the purpose of John 20, for example, is to tell us what happened. Something happened, to be sure, and that is important. But as we saw, John 20 seems more interested in getting us to linger over its careful portraits of how Mary and Peter and John responded, and eventually how the risen Jesus interacted with them.

The books by Johnson and Frei are my main recommended reference points for the kind of approach I have been setting forward. A book of essays that takes up these challenges and pursues them with regard to Jesus is *Seeking the Identity of Jesus*, edited by Beverly Roberts Gaventa and Richard B. Hays,[4] a sequel of sorts to the book mentioned earlier entitled *The Art of Reading Scripture*. For the practically useful suggestion that when we are reading the Gospels we should attend to what sorts of questions we are *expected* to ask, and the interesting results of what happens when we ask *unexpected* questions, I am indebted to the edifying and entertaining study of Mark Allan Powell, *Chasing the Eastern Star*, which represents also the most fun I have ever had reading a theological book.[5] His short follow-up is particularly good for preachers.[6]

---

4. Beverly Roberts Gaventa and Richard B. Hays, eds, *Seeking the Identity of Jesus: A Pilgrimage* (Grand Rapids: Eerdmans, 2008).

5. Mark Allan Powell, *Chasing the Eastern Star: Adventures in Biblical Reader-Response Criticism* (Louisville: Westminster John Knox, 2001).

6. See Mark Allan Powell, *What Do They Hear? Bridging the Gap*

Reading John

Finally, I should indicate where I have found most help in reading John specifically. As will by now be clear, books majoring on historical questions have been less helpful for this project of spiritual reading. Among commentaries, I enjoyed in particular Lincoln, *The Gospel According to St. John*, and Marianne Meye Thompson, *John*.[7] Shorter and more literary observations abound in R. Alan Culpepper's *The Gospel and Letters of John*.[8] The most stimulating book by far, though not because I necessarily find its approach always in line with what I have said here, was Sandra M. Schneiders's fascinating study *Written That You May Believe*.[9] This helped me to see many things that I would not naturally have looked for, some of which I ended up agreeing were important to see. I could go on listing fine and fortifying books, but instead will take a leaf out of John's own book and its ending: there is much more to say, the world cannot contain all the books that can be imagined, and we stop here.

Between Pulpit and Pew (Nashville: Abingdon, 2007).

7. Andrew T. Lincoln, *The Gospel According to St. John*, Black's New Testament Commentaries (London: Continuum, 2005); Marianne Meye Thompson, *John*, New Testament Library (Louisville: Westminster John Knox, 2015).

8. R. Alan Culpepper, *The Gospel and Letters of John*, Interpreting Biblical Texts (Nashville: Abingdon, 1998).

9. Sandra M. Schneiders, *Written That You May Believe: Encountering Jesus in the Fourth Gospel*, rev. and exp. ed (New York: Herder & Herder, 2003).

CLOSING CREDITS

In Others' Words

I THOUGHT IT WOULD be helpful if the readings of John in this book did not contain footnotes, that feature of academic writing that clogs up the page with references to other people's books, partly (one sometimes feels) in order for the author to draw attention to the various other books that they have read. The more noble reason for footnotes is to acknowledge a debt to other people's ideas, and sometimes to quote their best sentences word-for-word when you cannot think of a better way to say it yourself. Is that like the Gospel writers trying to describe Jesus, puzzling over how to do that, and then realizing that Isaiah or the Psalms had already done it amazingly well, and so using their words instead? Yes it is, in a way, although that is for another book.

Even so, some of my best ideas, as hard as this may be to believe, have also been had by many other people, including sometimes people who I read and was influenced by myself. So here, for the sake of integrity (and also incidentally to suggest some excellent further reading) is a brief rehearsal of where I learned many helpful and relevant things, as well as pointers to specific books that are mentioned or discretely followed in the readings offered. And there is also also a funny story or two, just to reward those who stay for the closing credits.

The concluding reflection at the end of the book explores some of my general reflections on useful resources for spiritual reading and John. For more specific points, I will take it chapter by chapter, though not every chapter is so particularly indebted that it needs referencing here.

In the introduction, I refer explicitly to the wonderful book by Alan Jacobs, *The Pleasures of Reading in an Age of Distraction*.[1] Anything by Alan Jacobs is itself a pleasure to read, and the "age of distraction" is indeed a real problem for our Bible reading. My own attempts to write something helpful on "hermeneutics," the science or art of reading well, include a book designed to introduce many of its different questions and challenges: *Reading the Bible Wisely*.[2] Those who would like to ponder more theoretically the question of what spiritual reading really is (and is not), as I put it in the introduction, might take a look at Lincoln, McConville, and Pietersen's *The Bible and Spirituality*.[3]

Chapter 1 does not quote Karl Barth, nor even work with anything specific that he said, but the idea that we start in and with Christ developed for me over several years of reading Barth. People wondering where to begin with his massive published works are still best pointed to his early sermon: "The Strange New World Within the Bible," in his *The Word*

---

1. Alan Jacobs, *The Pleasures of Reading in an Age of Distraction* (Oxford: Oxford University Press, 2011).

2. Richard Briggs, *Reading the Bible Wisely: An Introduction to Taking Scripture Seriously*, rev. ed (Eugene, OR: Cascade, 2011).

3. Andrew T. Lincoln, et al., eds, *The Bible and Spirituality: Exploratory Essays in Reading Scripture Spiritually* (Eugene, OR: Cascade, 2013).

of God and the Word of Man.[4] Regarding chapter 2, Jesus as the one who takes over the identity of the suffering servant, as Israel's mission becomes also the church's mission, is an established way for Christian Old Testament scholars to reflect on links between the Old and New Testaments. In my opinion, the most illuminating account of it is in a book by H. G. M. Williamson, *Variations on a Theme*.[5] Chapter 5 begins with noticing the similarity of "encounter with the woman at the well" scenes, known as "type scenes" ever since the master class in how to read this kind of narrative artistry that was offered by Robert Alter, *The Art of Biblical Narrative*.[6] His chapter on "Biblical Type-Scenes and the Uses of Convention" includes reference to this particular issue on pages 51–58, although the well as such is not essential to his discussion of "betrothal scenes."[7]

Chapter 6 is the most concentrated attempt to read a Gospel narrative in the "realistic" terms set out by Hans Frei, and discussed in my final reflections.[8] In the light of the approach taken by Frei, and discussed in my conclusion, it was sobering to turn to commentaries and discover how very little at all they said about the *point* of Jesus' walking on the water in John 6. In the end, I was most helped by a single paragraph and accompanying footnote in Richard B. Hays'

---

4. Karl Barth, "The Strange New World Within the Bible," in *The Word of God and the Word of Man*, edited by Douglas Horton, 28–50 (London: Hodder & Stoughton, 1928).

5. H. G. M Williamson, *Variations on a Theme: King, Messiah and Servant in the Book of Isaiah* (Carlisle: Paternoster, 1998).

6. Robert Alter, *The Art of Biblical Narrative* (London: Allen & Unwin, 1981).

7. Alter, *Art of Biblical Narrative*, 47–62.

8. See further Hans W. Frei, *The Identity of Jesus Christ: The Hermeneutical Bases of Dogmatic Theology* (Philadelphia: Fortress, 1975).

Echoes of Scripture in the Gospels.[9] Writing this chapter also allowed me to reflect on my own slightly traumatic attempt to have to sing the "Exsultet" on Easter morning during my own diaconal year in the Church of England. As it happened, my daughter, who is an excellent singer, was preaching her first sermon that same morning, as she celebrated the resurrection at a church in France. My wife reflected on how this seemed to add up to one of God's many examples of the divine sense of humor: how did it happen that on Easter morning I was singing in church while our daughter preached, and not the other way around? I am pleased to report that both congregations emerged unscathed.

Chapter 7 starts to explore some ideas about resurrection, which are taken up more fully in chapter 10 on John 20. That will be a good note on which to finish, so first let me get a proper acknowledgement out of the way, that chapter 9 quotes a line from the Rolling Stones' unusual song "You Can't Always Get What You Want," sung in part with the London Bach Choir (who allegedly did not know what context they were singing for until a copy of the *Let It Bleed* album arrived and somewhat disheartened them). In any case, this lament for the 1960s was written by Keith Richards and Mick Jagger, and released by the Rolling Stones in 1969.

Back to the resurrection in chapters 7 and 10. My understanding of resurrection was transformed (appropriately enough) by reading Jon D. Levenson's *Resurrection and the Restoration of Israel.*[10] This is the reason why chapter 10 emphasizes the line "resurrection is what it was always

---

9. Richard B. Hays, *Echoes of Scripture in the Gospels* (Waco: Baylor University Press, 2016). See especially 301 and 430n49.

10. Jon D. Levenson, *Resurrection and the Restoration of Israel: The Ultimate Victory of the God of Life* (New Haven: Yale University Press, 2006).

about"—it turns out that this is yet one more profound New Testament idea that the Old Testament had first, a phenomenon I find myself encountering time and again with Holy Scripture. Finally, chapter 7 also includes the passing observation that "Father Abraham had many sons" may have been written about Abraham Lincoln. This obscure suggestion, probably not much of a blessing to any youth groups enjoying performing it as an action song, is rather difficult to corroborate. The origins of the song may be lost, but mid-nineteenth-century songs in praise of "Father Abraham" (i.e., Abraham Lincoln) are indeed traceable, most notably "We are coming Father Abraham, three hundred thousand more" (or, in some versions, "a hundred thousand strong"), which I found in Richard Crawford's *The Civil War Songbook*.[11] Of course, astute readers will spot that on the terms I set out in this present book, it matters relatively little whether the song originally referred to Abraham Lincoln. That it serves to animate the faith of the young and the energetic in worship gatherings around the world is enough.

---

11. Richard Crawford, *The Civil War Songbook* (New York: Dover, 1977).

CPSIA information can be obtained
at www.ICGtesting.com
Printed in the USA
LVHW091829070819
626851LV00001BA/202/P